WHAT?

Teenagers in the Bible?

The Bible's Teens Speak to Teens Today

WHAT?

Teenagers in the Bible?

The Bible's Teens Speak to Teens Today

Sharon Norris Elliott

REDEMPTION
PRESS

ISBN 13: 978-1-63232-718-5
Library of Congress Catalog Card Number: 2003104047

Dedication

This book is dedicated to my sons, Matthew and Mark,
because of their unconditional love for me,
and their understanding as I took time at the computer to write;
and
to my students at South Bay Lutheran High School
in Inglewood, California,
because of their encouragement
and the way they would catch my excitement
as I talked about God's word.

May you all come to enjoy
the people in the Bible
as much as I do,
and learn from them how
to enjoy the Lord.

Special Thanks to . . .

. . . James, my encourager, my wonderful husband. Your support has made this book, and many of my other dreams, come true.

. . . The faculties and staffs of Mount Hermon, Sandy Cove, and Glorieta Christian Writers' Conferences, and CLASServices. You all have never failed to pray for me and urge me on as I traveled along my writing journey.

. . . Jessica Shaver and Kathy Collard Miller. Your unflinching belief in the gifts God gave me has inspired me time and time again. You saw the raw material and prayed me through the beginning of the refining process. You have my gratitude for having something uplifting to say every time we've connected through the years.

. . . Saundra, Cheryl, Meloni, Jean, Mary, Michele, Diana, Shalawnda, Dawn, and Tammy. You are my "girls", my incredible "fan club" of encouragement. You tolerate hearing about every new writing idea. You've cheered me through the process of getting this one written and published. I love you ladies and can't imagine life without you.

. . . My remarkable critique group. You've read and torn apart tons of my manuscripts, showing absolutely no mercy. You are an integral part of my writing career and success.

. . . My student, Walter Parham, for the title of this book.

. . . All the teenagers I have ever taught. You are the main reason this book exists. You keep my outlook fresh, my vocabulary up-to-date, and my ego humble. I love you guys.

Table of Contents

Chapter 1: 11
Chapter 2: Impulsive 15
Chapter 3: Unconcerned 23
Chapter 4: Naive 33
Chapter 5: Lazy 41
Chapter 6: Daring 49
Chapter 7: Dishonest 57
Chapter 8: No Discernment 65
Chapter 9: Impressionable 73
Chapter 10: Stubborn 81
Chapter 11: Disrespectful 91
Chapter 12: Undisciplined 99
Chapter 13: Not Taken Seriously 107
Chapter 14: Impatient 115
Chapter 15: Headstrong 123

The teen years—what a great time of life, but what a weird time of life as well. If we looked way back through history, I think we would find that teens throughout the ages have always tried to express their independence through their dances, clothing, and sayings. Just peak at the past thirty years or so to see just how much your wonderful age group has affected society.

Teenagers in the 1960's were doing a dance called "The Go-Go" and were wearing thigh-level go-go boots, white lipstick, and flowered pants. Teens in the 70's wore afros or ironed hairstyles, polyester bell-bottoms, letterman jackets, wallabee shoes or platforms as they danced "The Hustle" or "The Bump" in a disco. In the 80's, teens danced "The Electric Slide" in skin-tight jeans. The 90's found teenagers dancing "The Lambada," "The Macarena," "The Totsy Roll," and "The Butterfly" in baggy, unisex clothes that are open in select places to show their tattoos or body piercings.

And what about teen language? When adults said something was "good" in the 1960's, teens said it was "cool". In the 70's, "good" was "bad"; in the 80's, "good" was "fresh," and in the 90's, "good" was "all that," "off the hook," or "the bomb". Descriptions of the negative were no less confusing. When adults said something wasn't nice, 60's teens said that was "a bad scene"; 70's teens called it "messed up"; 80's teens felt "dis-ed"; and 90's teens simply "didn't go there".

Shock value seems to drive your fads from generation to generation. The secret teenage creed must go something like this:

On my honor, I will try; To be as different from adults as is humanly possible. If adults like what I'm doing, THERE MUST BE SOMETHING WRONG WITH IT!

But fads must change. Teenagers eventually become adults and you, as the upcoming teens, have to come up with different hair styles, fashion trends, dances, even vocabulary, in an effort to find out who you really are.

Yes, the teen years are a weird time of life. You're too old to be treated like a little kid, yet you're too young to have any real freedom. When the note the choir soprano hits strikes you funny in church, someone is quick to shoot a frown at you and warn, "Stop acting like a child." Then, when you have some great input for the discussion around the Thanksgiving table, you're cut short with the words, "Children should be seen and not heard." What are you supposed to do? Who are you supposed to be?

You, like thousands of teens everywhere, are asking that question daily. You are searching—searching for your identity and your independence. Your other favorite questions all begin with the word, "Why?" and your favorite response to any rule is, "Why not?"

Perhaps you have tried asking other people for answers to these questions about yourself. You may have talked it over with your friends, sisters or brothers, or—wonder of wonders—your parents or some other adult. If you have, I'm willing to bet that you received as many different answers as people you asked.

The advise you get from people reflects how they feel about you and about teenagers in general. I recently found out just how wide of a variety of opinions about teenagers exists among adults I know. Here are some of the answers I got when I asked them to complete this sentence: Teenagers are . . .

Chapter 1

Boisterous	Observant
Confused	Overbearing
Easy	Pressured
Energetic	Put down
Excessive	Shameless
Exuberant	Silly
Fake	Spontaneous
Free-spirited	Stereotyped
Frustrated	Strong-willed
Hopeful	Sweet
Indecisive	Unappreciated
Irritating	Ungrateful
Loud	Weak
More intelligent than they seem	

As you can see, there are about an equal amount of positive and negative comments about teens, depending upon your understanding of what each word means. How would you complete the statement? Be honest. Take a moment now to think of ten words or short phrases you would use to complete the same sentence: Teenagers are . . .

_____   _____

_____   _____

_____   _____

_____   _____

_____   _____

As you embark upon or continue your search for who you are supposed to be, I'd like you to use this book to help you see yourself in a new way. I want you to see yourself not as adults see you, not as the media, the government, or any establishment sees you. I'd like you to see yourself as God sees you.

God created you. It was His idea to make the life cycle turn in such a way that everyone who makes it to age 20 must pass through Teenagerville—the ages of 13 through 19. You arrive at the gates of Teenagerville right around your 13th birthday. At the gates, it seems as though you receive certain characteristics (traits, qualities, attributes). Your task during your journey through town, which will end on your 20th birthday, is to master the correct use of these characteristics. If you figure out their correct use, you exit Teenagerville as a well-balanced young adult, well on your way to emotional and spiritual maturity. If you misuse them—well, let's just say that you could get very used to the term "dysfunctional".

This book will explore 14 mostly negative characteristics commonly used to describe you as a teenager. Surprisingly, teenagers in the Bible had to struggle with these same years of confusion and I'm sure they had the same questions about identity that you now have. They had opportunities to use or misuse the same qualities you deal with. (After all, King Solomon did say, "There is nothing new under the sun" Eccl. 1:9 (NIV).)

Some of these teens made the wrong choices and the negative characteristic caused them all sorts of trouble. Other Bible teens made the right choices and turned their negative teen reputation into a positive trait they were able to carry with them into adulthood.

So, as you read, I'd like for you to focus on three things. First, notice the many different ways these Bible teenagers were just like you and your friends. Second, watch how these Bible teens handled their unique situations. Finally, ask yourself how you can make the Bible teens' positive traits part of your own life.

Now, I'd like to introduce you to some Bible teens who are remarkably just like you.

Impulsive

DAVID

1 Sam. 16 and 17:17ff
I will not run from Goliath.

Being the youngest in the family has its advantages and its disadvantages. The good part is how you seem to get away with things that your older brothers and sisters never could have dreamed of pulling off. Your parents have gotten used to telling the older kids, "Leave the baby alone." But, there's a down side. Watching everyone else have all the fun and having to miss out because you're too young is messed up. You are sick of hearing, "You're not old enough yet," or "Your time will come before you know it." You're the one they pick on, tease, and overprotect. You may have even learned to play alone or just hang by yourself, entertaining yourself with elaborate make-believe adventures and extraordinary plans.

My name is David and I can identify with you. I was the youngest in a family full of handsome, strong, popular boys. I ended up with the whack job of watching the stupid, smelly sheep. When

15

my brothers all went off to serve honorably in King Saul's army, there I sat—in the fields with the boring sheep.

I was a good shepherd. I was smart enough and strong enough to kill a lion and a bear all by myself to protect my flock. Still, watching the dumb sheep couldn't possibly compare to what I imagined my brothers must be doing out on the front lines of Israel's army. That's where the real stuff was happening.

So I could hardly believe it when my dad sent me to go see how my brothers were doing out on the line. I would finally get a peak at the action. It was really a trip when I got there because what I saw was way different than what I had expected to see.

Just as I walked up, I heard the mighty Philistine champion, Goliath, challenge the Israelite army to send out one man to fight him. Goliath's deal was that whoever won between him and the Israeli champion would prove that his side was best. The losing side would then serve the winning side.

"All right, what luck," I thought. "I got here just in time to see everything go down." What I didn't know was that this challenge had been being made for the past few days. I looked on in shocked disbelief as I witnessed the Israelite army punking out in front of this 9-foot bully. This 'being scared' stuff just isn't the way things are supposed to be going.

"God's army doesn't run from anybody," I thought. "Somebody's got to do something!"

Just then my brothers tried to hurry me home. They acted like they only wanted to protect me, but I knew they didn't want me to see them being wimps.

"Go on home, kid. This is not place for a shrimp like you," they urged.

I guess my teenage impulsiveness kicked in because, without even thinking I shouted, "I'll fight that bully!"

"Yeah, right. What do you think you're going to do against Goliath? Look at him. He'll eat you alive."

"Look, he's not just challenging you," I argued. "By calling you out, he's calling God out and God can't lose. Let me at him."

Impulsive

Well, nobody else was volunteering, so to my surprise, I was escorted to the king and my proposal was presented to Saul. The king probably figured, "I know this much, this kid's got spunk."

Before I knew it, there I was, standing face to knee-cap with Goliath. While Goliath mouthed off about how he'd win the fight, I used that impulsiveness everybody kept saying I had, to my advantage once again. I ran full speed toward Goliath, launched one stone from my sling shot, and hit the bragging giant squarely in the forehead. The stone (no doubt helped by God's hand) sunk in, Goliath swayed, and **CRASH**, down he fell in a cloud of dust.

Lots of times, you defend your honor without even thinking about it. You don't let anybody get away with talking about you. You usually take no thought of whether or not you can take the other person. You just straighten folks out right away, not even considering that your words or actions could get you into trouble more times than not.

David's whole motivation for impulsively approaching Goliath was the fact that Goliath had the nerve to challenge God.

The impulsiveness God has given you doesn't have to be a negative trait. Like David, it's okay to be impulsive about what God wants you to do. When there's opposition to your faith, move quickly to defend God's honor. This obviously means that you'll have to be alert and you'll have to be able to recognize when God's honor is being attacked.

What would you do if you found yourself in the following situations? How could you defend God's honor and not back down from "Goliath"?

- A science teacher presents the theory of evolution as a fact and then asks the class for discussion.

- You are approached by members of the Nation of Islam who tell you that Christianity is the white man's religion and it exists to keep the Black man in a servant's role.

- The popular kids at school invite you to join a club that meets every Sunday morning at 9:30 A.M. This is the same time you are normally in church.

17

- You have decided to stop listening to any popular music that degrades women, encourages violence, endorses pre-marital sex, or contains curse words. Then, for your birthday, one of your friends gives you an expensive, very popular CD that has the elements in it you have eliminated from you collection. When your friend asks you how you liked the gift, what do you say?

- Your favorite uncle fixes you up with a blind date. In the middle of the date, you find out that this person is not a Christian and is very vocal about his/her belief that God doesn't exist at all.

David chose not to run from Goliath. He courageously held his ground when nobody believed in him and the situation looked pretty hopeless. He was tuned in to the Holy Spirit and used his teenage impulsiveness to carry out God's plan for his life for that moment. Give your impulsive nature to the Lord and watch Him use you in exciting ways to let others see Jesus in you.

Impulsive

DO THIS: This week, listen closely to the conversations and comments of your friends, teachers, and family members. Keep a record of how the comments you hear present a wrong view of God and/or morality. Write down the comment and what was wrong about what was said. Then, if you're ready to face some Goliaths, respond to whatever their comment is.

<u>Examples</u> (lines one and two):

Person	Comment	What's Wrong With That?	Response
Physical Education teacher	Sex is okay between two mature people who love each other.	Sex between unmarried people is sin.	I said, "Only if those two people are married to each other.
Tremaine Wilson - friend	Tiffany is better off since she had that abortion. She wasn't ready to raise a baby anyway. She's only 15.	Abortion kills babies.	I said, "Tiffany could have put the baby up for adoption. She will probably feel worse now that she's killed her baby.

NOW DO THIS: On this new chart below, write in the names of the television shows you like to watch. Then for one week, keep a record of the comments made in those shows that present a wrong view of God and/or morality. At the end of the week, review the chart and come up with a justifiable reason for why you watch the shows that present God and/or morality in unbiblical ways.

TV Show Title	Comment Made On The Show	What's Wrong With That? (Biblically)	My Reason for Continuing to Watch This Show

Memory Verse For "Impulsive David"

Prov. 3:26 For the LORD will be your confidence, and will keep your foot from being caught. (NAS)

Chapter 3

Unconcerned

Mary

Luke 1:26–56, Matt. 1:18–24, Luke 2:1–50
I will not worry about God's plan for me (or I will not sweat it).

I was just going through life, minding my own business on the morning that it all started. All of a sudden, I turned around, and this big guy was standing in my room. But this guy wasn't like any of the guys who lived here in Nazareth. I thought Joseph, my handsome fiancé, was tall, but this dude stood way taller. His shoulders were broader, his biceps were rounder, and well, he was just the biggest dude I had ever seen.

"Hi, Mary," he said. "When it comes to you and the other girls around town—let's see, how can I say this so you'll understand—you're the bomb."

He must have seen the fear and confusion in my eyes because he immediately continued to babble on.

"Don't be afraid. Check this out. I'm here to tell you that God is really pleased with you. He has decided that you are going to be the mother of His son."

My knees got weak then and I got a little light-headed. I think he reached out to help me as I sank to sit down on the edge of my bed, but I'm not sure because my mind was racing. First of all, this guy must be an angel or something if he was sent from God and could just appear in my room out of nowhere. Secondly, I was hearing his message but could it be true? I had been taught all my life that the Messiah, the One who would provide salvation for my people the Jews, would be born and it was logically accepted that some Jewish young woman would be the one to be His mother. We also knew that this special child had to be born to a direct descendent of King David. My family, especially my old Aunt Ruth, proudly bragged about the fact that we could trace our line straight back to the king. Now, with my being engaged to Joseph who was also a descendent, my friends really like to daydream and tease me.

Every now and then, when my friends and I got together while drawing water at the well, the subject of the Messiah's birth would come up.

"Mary, it really could be you, you know," they'd say. "You've got all the credentials and the qualities. Wouldn't that be a trip?"

"Yeah," I'd answer. "But who would believe me? What am I supposed to say? What would you guys do if I came out here one morning and announced, 'Hey, it's me. I'm going to be the mother of the Lord!' "

Everybody would explode in laughter. "I guess you're right," my friends would answer. "There must be hundreds of girls who are in King David's line who we don't even know. Besides, how much sense does it make for the Messiah to come out of a little hick town like Nazareth?"

Secretly, we all wanted to be the one chosen but we didn't want to sound like we did. We'd go on discussing it excitedly, always in hushed tones, because we didn't want anybody to think we were crazy. And now, here was this guy—this angel—saying the Messiah's mother really would be me! I couldn't believe it.

This guy didn't seem to be bothered about my being in shock though. I guess he may not have known how I felt because I pretty much keep my feelings inside. I don't like to go off about stuff. I see it this way, why trip out when you don't even have all the facts and whatever you're trippin' over may not happen anyway. My parents probably think I just don't care about anything, but it's not that. I'm just taking my time and checking everything out, and this story demanded that I do some hard thinking.

"Okay, here's how this whole plan is going to work." This guy in my room started talking again and brought me back to reality. "You are going to be pregnant, you'll have a boy, and you'll name Him Jesus. Your son will be great. Actually, He'll be God's own Son and God intends to give Him David's throne."

I think I pretty much missed everything in his speech after he said, "You are going to be pregnant," I wasn't even married. It was time for me to speak up.

"Wait a minute. Did I hear you right?" I asked. "How can I be pregnant? I've never messed around. I'm a virgin and proud of it."

"Not a problem," he responded. "God, through the Holy Spirit, is going to cause your pregnancy by His power. That's why your baby will be known as the Son of God."

What more was there to say? Anyway, what good would it do to argue with God? I sure didn't want to make Him mad. But I still must have looked a little unsure because the angel put the clincher on his speech.

"Okay look. You know your relative Elizabeth, right?"

I wondered silently, "What did she have to do with this?"

"You know how she's wanted a baby all her life. Well, now she and Zacharias are very old, but check it out. Elizabeth is six months pregnant herself. Now, you tell me, is anything too hard for God?"

That's all I needed to hear. It was a lot to take in at once, but I couldn't worry about that. There were many practical things to consider. For example, what was Joseph going to say? He'd probably think I was messing around with some other guy and was just trying to get sympathy with this angel story. Then, even if Joseph did believe me, how would we explain this pregnancy to our families? Most of all, how were we going to dodge the law that said I should be stoned (that's killed) because I was pregnant out of wedlock?

My mind went back into its laid-back mode. "Hey," I thought, "I'm only 14 years old and I can't be bothered with the details. I figure, as long as I remember that this is God's baby, God's plan, and what God wants me to do, everything will be cool."

Look through a current high school yearbook. Teenagers are very cool. Check out the senior portraits and sports photos. Lots of them, especially the pictures of the guys, are posed with no smiles. It's just not the thing to do, to show your emotions. That's why it comes across like they're so unconcerned. It looks like they don't care about much of anything.

I remember an episode of <u>The Cosby Show</u> in which Theo, the 16-year-old son, showed this teenage trait of seeming to be unconcerned. He had never been fishing before so his dad took him. However, instead of catching a fish, Theo fished up a dead body which, it turned out, belonged to an infamous underworld crime figure. His reaction at the lake was stark fear, but like the 'one-that-got-away' stories, Theo's bravery grew over time. By the time he was being interviewed by the evening news, his recollection had been distilled to the cool statement, "I'm taking it all in stride".

Mary seemed relatively unconcerned about this situation in which she found herself. She asked the angel only one question and then she was okay.

You too can use your unconcern to your advantage as a Christian. Phil. 4:6–7 says that God's peace can flood your heart and your mind when you give your troubles to God in prayer. You're used to kickin' back, so keep that kick back trait alive when problems come your way.

Once you realize that God's word has an answer for anything you might face, your unconcerned attitude can then become discernment. Discernment is the ability to look at a situation and make the wisest choice as to the action you should take. When you are discerning, you are able to calmly sit back, check everything out, and then be honest about evaluating what you see. To increase your ability to discern, you do need a working knowledge of the teachings of the Bible. How else will you know whether or not you have made the wisest choice unless you know what God has said about the issue?

DO THIS: Check your discernment. How would you handle the following situations? Answer for yourself first, then look up the Scripture and see how God would have you handle it. No cheating now. Fill in your answer first—preferably in ink, then look up God's answers.

1.   You meet this really nice guy/girl at school. You discover over the next few weeks that he/she likes all the same things you like—same movies, music, food, clothing styles. You even have the same opinions about drugs, friends, and sex. You start dating and everything's cool until you invite him/her to your church. He/She responds by saying, "Sure, I'll check out your church if you'll begin to chant with me. My religion feels that every religion is all right."

What's your reaction?

WHAT I WOULD DO	WHAT GOD WOULD DO
	John 14:6
	2 Cor. 6:14

2. You go to a party with some friends. The same people with whom you rode drink alcohol at the party. They say that you can be their designated driver so that everyone can get home safely. You just finished your driver's class and will be going to DMV to get your license this coming Saturday.

WHAT I WOULD DO	WHAT GOD WOULD DO
	Eph. 5:18
	Ps. 15

3. It's time for final exams. You have struggled through your history class and you have to do well on the final to get a decent grade in the course. Your transcripts have to look good in order for you to get that college scholarship. Suddenly the phone rings and startles you back to reality. You answer and it's your friend, Mike. He informs you that he just happens to have, in his possession, a copy of the history final. He says there are lots of questions on it about stuff the teacher didn't go over too much. Mike offers you a copy of the exam for $5.

WHAT I WOULD DO	WHAT GOD WOULD DO
	Ex. 20:15
	I Thess. 4:11

4. You have fooled around in almost every class this semester and now it's report card time. You know your parents are going to go off when they see your grades. Then you realize that there is at least one period that you will pass and that's "Office Aide". And as the office aide, you also realize that you have access to the school computer. You know that the teachers post their grades by 3 P.M. Tuesday, but report cards aren't printed until Thursday morning. It would be really easy to log on during your Office Aide period on Wednesday and do a little grade changing.

WHAT I WOULD DO	WHAT GOD WOULD DO
	Prov. 19:5
	Eph. 6:2

Mary chose not to let strange circumstances cause her too much concern. She used discernment and evaluated the situation. She did her part and her part only and allowed God to do His part without her interference or her worry. Turn your unconcerned nature over to the Lord and watch Him give you peaceful insight into His great ability.

NOW DO THIS: Write down actual situations that happen over the next two weeks that require you to think about what God wants you to do. Write the situation and how God helped you respond.

Situation	How I Handled It

MEMORY VERSE FOR "UNCONCERNED MARY"

Phil 4:6–7 Do not be anxious about anything, but in everything, by prayer and petition, with thanksgiving, present your requests to God. And the peace of God, which transcends all understanding, will guard your hearts and your minds in Christ Jesus. (NIV)

Chapter 4

Naive

ISAAC

Gen. 21–22:19
I will not neglect the faith of my father.

Hi, I'm Isaac and I'm like some of you. My parents believe in God and I was brought up believing God exists. I never really challenged that either. Call me naive if you like, but it made sense to me that there was a God. God had done so much for my parents that I just hoped I was good enough for Him to be that way toward me. My dad would tell me about lots of times when God came through for him, including the miracle of my birth.

Mom and Dad (Abraham and Sarah) prayed for years for a child. Since God had given Dad a promise that he would have many, many descendants, that seemed like a pretty safe prayer to pray to which they could be assured of getting a "yes" answer. But, as the years went by and they still didn't have a baby, Mom got desperate. She decided to take advantage of a rule used by some of the people they had met in their travels. She could let one of her servants become pregnant by my dad and then, since she owned the servant, she would own the baby. In other words, her servant's baby would legally be her child. I guess you could call it a surrogate pregnancy situation.

Okay, so Mom picked Hagar, her Egyptian handmaiden, to be the surrogate. Dad didn't complain and the next thing you know, Hagar was pregnant. Mom obviously thought this would be cool, but she and Hagar ended up hating one another behind this baby. Hagar paraded her big belly in front of Mom making her feel bad that she wasn't pregnant herself, and Mom actually got jealous. When Mom went to my dad for help, Dad just said, "I'm not in it. This was your big idea, you handle it."

Mom handled it all right. She got so deep with Hagar that the woman ran away. I guess they just needed the time and Dad says that God got through to both of them, because Hagar came back. She had her baby with Mom right there and, although Hagar was still around to help with the baby, Mom immediately took over as my brother Ishmael's mother.

Everything seemed like it had worked until 13 years later when the Lord visited Dad and told him that he and Mom would have their own baby. By this time, Dad was 100 years old and Mom was 90. They had long since stopped praying for their own son. After all, they were counting Ishmael as their kid.

"Thanks God," Dad said humbly, "but we've got Ishmael. Just let him stand before You."

"No," said the Lord. "Your offspring will come from the bodies of you and your wife Sarah."

Mom was eavesdropping on this whole conversation. "Yeah, right," she thought. "There's no way this dried-up old body is going to have a baby now." She couldn't help laughing.

The Lord asked, "Why did Sarah laugh?"

Mom came out. "I didn't laugh," she denied.

"Yes you did. Be assured that at this time next year, you will be holding your own baby in your arms. And be sure to name him Isaac because that means laughter."

Well, sure enough, there I came about that time the very next year. Mom and Dad were extremely proud and thankful, and my big brother, Ishmael, would play with me. Of course, I thought everything fine. Then one day, Ishmael was clowning around and Mom caught him teasing me. She got mad. Really mad.

"Ishmael," she yelled, "I've had just about enough of you. You are forever clowning around and now you have turned your sick sense of humor on my son. How dare you."

Ishmael didn't know quite what to say. It wasn't that he was upset because she was yelling at him. Kids get used to being yelled at. It's what she said and the way she had said it. "My son," she had said, referring only to me and not to him. That really hurt. All he could do was stare at Mom.

Dad had walked up on the scene and so had Hagar. Ishmael's staring just made Mom more mad. Mom turned to Dad and complained, "I don't think they can stay here any longer. Isaac is the heir, the one who will inherit the belongings and the blessing of God from you." Mom's eyes were wild. I may have been little, but I remember the strange look on her face. "The son of this maid is not going to complicate these issues. It's time for them to leave."

Dad didn't know what to do. He loved Ishmael as his own son. Well, Ishmael *was* his own son.

Later Dad told me that, as he did with everything else, he immediately prayed. God told Dad to go on and tell Hagar and Ishmael that they had to go. But, He also promised Dad that He would take special care of them. Since Ishmael was Dad's son, God promised to make a nation out of him too.

I didn't understand it all at the time. All I knew was that my big brother was gone and sometimes I got lonely until I got used to the idea that he wasn't ever coming back. We've heard since then that Hagar and Ishmael found another life and they're cool. Still, the whole incident was a trip.

Anyway, so it was now only me to be raised by my mom and dad and get all of their attention. If you're an only child, you may know how it feels to get all that attention. Sometimes it's okay, sometimes it's not. It's cool when you're the only one on holidays who they have to buy gifts for. You can pretty much clean up if you've kept your act together. But at other times, you feel the pressure of being the only one they're depending on to make them proud and to have all the opportunities they didn't have when they were your age.

Most of the time though, it was pretty cool. I used to really like the times when Dad and I would go on our camping trips. We would go up into the mountains, hunt, talk, pray, and sacrifice to the Lord. I was around 15 or 16 when one of those camping trips turned a little strange.

This camping/sacrifice trip had started out like any other. We headed toward Mt. Moriah with a donkey loaded down with the wood we'd need to build the altar. The assistants who usually went with us were all ready, early as usual. It would be about a week-long trip and I was excited.

By the third day, we had made it to the foot of Mt. Moriah. Then God did an unusual thing.

"Stay here," Dad told the assistants. "Isaac and I will go up the mountain alone to worship. Just wait for us here and we'll return to you soon."

That was strange. The assistants always went with us because Dad wanted them to know how to worship his God. No sooner had I finished trippin' on that, that I noticed something else. We didn't have an animal with us to sacrifice to the Lord.

"Dad," I asked. "We have the fire and the wood, but where is the animal we're going to use for the burnt offering?"

"God will give us the sacrifice, my son," he answered.

He didn't seem to be worried about it, so all I could say was, "Okay."

We hiked on together for about an hour until we found a perfect place to build an altar. Dad wanted to do most of the work building the altar this time and he seemed really deep in thought about something. I didn't bother him, but just kept myself busy handing Dad what he needed to build the altar.

When the altar was finished, I figured it was time to go hunting for an animal to sacrifice. Instead, Dad called me over to him. Without saying anything, he took the rope and started tying me up. He tied my hands and feet just like we would have tied a lamb before we sacrificed it. I was confused and a little scared, but as I looked into Dad's eyes, I could tell that he was doing something God was telling him to do. Although I didn't understand it, I knew that look and when he had that look on his face, there was nothing anyone could say to change his mind about whatever he was doing.

Dad then picked me up and laid me on the altar. Tears were streaming down his cheeks as he looked up toward heaven and raised a knife over me. All of a sudden, Dad stopped, seemed to be listening to something I couldn't hear, then he used the knife to untie my hands and feet. We then saw a ram, caught by its horns, in a nearby thicket. Why we didn't see it before, I don't know, but there it was. We caught it and offered that ram to the Lord instead of offering me.

As we were traveled down the mountain to meet the assistants, Dad told me what I had not known about the whole trip.

"Isaac," he began. "God told me to take this trip with you."

"He usually does, Dad," I replied.

"Yes son, but this time God told me to sacrifice you as a burnt offering."

"Why?"

"I didn't know why at first either. I just knew that I had to do what God said for me to do. I wondered and worried the whole day. With Ishmael gone, how could God take you from me too? It was too strange. I knew God had something in mind, but I had no idea what it was. How could He be asking me to kill the son I love so much?"

We walked a little further before he could continue.

"Well, I couldn't have the assistants see me kill you. They would have tried to stop me and I had to go through with what God had said. Once you were tied and on top of the altar, I thought it was too late. I raised the knife and then the angel of the Lord called to me. I heard his voice as clearly as I hear you. He said, 'Do not stretch out your hand against your son. Now I know you really love me because you would not even withhold your only son from me.'"

"So you mean it was all a test?" I asked in surprise.

"Yes, that's right son. It was a test for me, but I see it was also a test for you."

"How, Dad?"

"You proved to me that you trust me and the God I have taught you to serve. I know that everything will be all right as you continue to grow into a man. Look at how faithful and amazing our God is.

"Yeah Dad. We know what He's like, but I guess He had to find out if we really loved Him like we say we do. I've seen how God has done stuff in your life, Dad. I plan to always trust God too. You passed your test, Dad."

"Son," Dad replied, "we both passed, today. We both passed."

It is important to realize that, even if you were raised in Church, you have to have your own relationship with God. It is wonderful to know God because your parents knew Him. If your parents are Christians, it was their job to make sure you understood who God was. You are not naive for believing what you have been taught. Still, by the time you are in your teens, you are old enough to start taking on the responsibility of maturing in your faith. Be thankful for what your Christian parents taught you, embrace those wonderful lessons, and keep them close to your heart.

DO THIS: List some things you learned from your parents about their faith in God. Beside each item, write down a short scenario to help you to remember and incident that taught you this lesson.

Things I learned from my parents about their faith in God	Scenario that taught me this lesson
Example: Dad believed God could be understood, seen, known in and through everyday situations.	Example: During car trips, Dad would have us write down sermon topics based on special things we would see or experience.

MEMORY VERSE FOR "NAIVE ISAAC"

Prov. 6:20–23 My son, keep your father's commands and do not forsake your mother's teaching. Bind them upon your heart forever; fasten them around your neck. When you walk, they will guide you; when you sleep, they will watch over you; when you awake, they will speak to you. For these commands are a lamp, this teaching is a light, and the corrections of discipline are the way to life. (NIV)

Chapter 5

Lazy

THE PRODIGAL SON

Luke 15:11–32
I will not work for a living.

I'm not going to tell you my name, but I guarantee you that you will be able to identify with me. Like you, I'm a teenager, and possibly like you, I came to the place where I was sick of my dad. I would get together with my friends and we'd talk about how fed up we were with our parents—all those rules, a constant hassle. My dad had me running errands, getting stuff for him, cleaning around the house, working late in the family business (and not getting paid for it), everything. And then his thing was, "And you'd better have a good attitude about it. I've worked hard all my life, yada, yada, yada . . . " But no matter how much I complained, I always went back home and right back to the rut I had come to hate. Well, talk is cheap, so I decided to do something about it.

I thought about it for a long time. I didn't want to be a punk and just run away. That was the chicken way out. Besides, I'd have to have somewhere to run and like I said before, all my friends had the same problems I had. It would have done me no good to go to live with one of them. My only option was to move out and take care of myself.

I know you have probably thought about that too and you just said, "Forget that," because you don't have a job paying good enough money to get you by. I considered that obstacle too. Then I had a brainstorm. My dad was pretty well off and when he died, my brother and I were going to get a pretty nice inheritance. *Why should I have to wait and why should I do backbreaking work for what's already mine?* I thought. My dad was real strong, a health food nut, in fact. It would take him years to die.

I started thinking harder. *I'm going to be old myself before I get that money, probably too old to even enjoy that inheritance. Besides, was my dad really handling my money right? Would it be as much as I'm thinking? Dad is pretty old-fashioned. He's not up-to-date on the newest and best ways to invest his money. As long as he has my money, he has control of my life.*

I was sick of his rules, sick of all the chores, sick of being his flunky. I was convinced that I was just basically sick of his control over my existence. It was a long shot, but I knew what I had to do. I got my rap together, found my dad in the den, and asked him if I could talk to him. He put down what he was working on and gave me his attention.

"Dad, I'm old enough to take care of myself now. You don't have to worry about me or carry me any longer. I'm going to live my own life. All you have to do is give me the portion of the inheritance that belongs to me and I'm out of here."

My dad looked at me for a long time. I wasn't sure whether he was going to blow up or what, so I braced myself for the worst. Finally, very calmly, he said, "Well you know son, that means I'll have to sell off some assets. You can't take buildings with you and livestock will slow you down. I will have to sell some of these things and turn them into cash in order to give you your portion of the estate. That may take a little time."

"Do what you have to do, Dad," I said. "I've made up my mind and I'm ready to go."

Again, my dad looked at me for a long time. I couldn't really read his eyes, but there was something new there I had never seen before. He didn't look mad. The look was actually a sort of mix between confusion, sadness, disbelief, and hurt. I shrugged it off though. I couldn't think emotionally right now. I was too far into this and I wanted to show him that I was a man who could make my own decisions, so I stood tough. Finally he said softly, "All right son. I'll liquidate those assets as quickly as possible."

It actually didn't take my dad as long as I thought it would. He came to me not long after with a pouch in his hand.

"Son," he said, "here's your portion of the estate. I have divided everything equitably as it would have been divided had I died and left it all to you and your brother." He paused to give me that strange look again. Then he just said, "So I guess you'll be leaving now."

With that, he turned and went into the den and closed the door.

I stood there for a while, trying to take in what had just happened. Suddenly, I held my freedom in my hands. I had thousands in that pouch. It was so hard to believe that I thought I was in a dream. But no, this was real. I could really start my life now.

I went to my room and started packing, then I realized, *Why am I taking all these old clothes into my new life? This is schoolboy stuff. I'll just take enough to get me where I'm going, then I'll buy all new clothes.*

I was at the door with my one bag and my pouch in less than an hour. "I'm gone," I yelled back into the house as I stood with my hand on the front door knob. No one answered. I knew my dad must have heard me because the den was just a few feet away. No matter. I guess he figured he had already said his good-byes and he was probably busy with the books again. *I'm glad I'm getting away from that mess*, I thought. *Who would want to spend the rest of his life with his nose buried in accounting books? You'd never get a chance to enjoy life.* There was no way I was going to miss out on everything coming to me. I was free. I walked out of that house and didn't even look back.

I traveled until I got to the biggest city in the region. Even though I had heard the tradesmen speak of it, I must admit that I wasn't ready for all the noise and the constant activity. It seemed like nobody ever went to sleep. Businesses were open from early in the morning until late at night. Then there was the night life. My dad had never let my brother or me come to the city before, and now I knew why. He knew that if we ever got here, we'd never return to the land to work with him. As far as my first impression went, he was right. Who would ever want to leave all this excitement?

I checked into a room at a hotel right near the center of town—near the center of all the action. On my first day there, I made friends while I was just walking around getting used to the area. I invited them to my hotel room for later that night and said I would throw a little get-together that night. News of the party traveled fast because my little room was packed with people. I had to re-order more food and drinks five times. It was off-the-hook!

Over the next couple of weeks, I met more people and threw more parties. I was Mr. Popular. Even the ladies loved me. Of course I treated the ladies to a few little gifts every now and then and they seemed to keep coming from everywhere. I was partying with all of them because I simply couldn't decide which beauty I wanted to be with and they didn't seem to mind sharing me. Life was good.

It only took a couple of months for me to run out of the money my dad had given me. It sure seemed like all that money would have gone a lot farther and frankly, I have no idea what I did with most of it and I certainly didn't have anything to show for it. I tried getting in touch with all those "friends" who had been coming to my parties. Funny thing. None of them had time for me now that I was broke. Nobody even offered me a place to stay when I couldn't pay for the hotel room any more. My situation was becoming very messed up, very fast.

When I couldn't find anybody to help me, I tried to find a job. Of course, I started applying for the cushion-y office jobs. Everywhere I tried said the same thing, "You need experience." How was I supposed to get experience if no one would hire me? Then I tried for retail work. A few seemed promising at first, but they said I needed a more conservative look. All the clothes I had bought were for parties, not for the work place. How was I supposed to afford appropriate clothes if I didn't have a job?

I was getting desperate. I didn't want to end up begging out on the street. Finally I got a job feeding this guy's pigs. I had to lug huge buckets of slop—corn cobs, potato peels, and other garbage—from the barn to the pig pen. Then I had to literally get into the pig pen to dump the buckets. Those pigs didn't wait for me to get out of there either before they crowded in to gobble down that stuff. I had to pick my way through it and around them to get to the gate that would get me out of there.

One day, those pigs and their greedy behinds knocked me face-first into their slop. They kept right on eating and I was so hungry, that I almost started chowing down on a corn cob or two myself. Then it hit me. I know I was talking to myself, but I didn't care.

"I can't believe this. Nobody is giving me any play. My father's servants have food enough to throw away and here I am starving to death. I'm going back to my dad. I'll say to him, 'I messed up; I was lazy and I messed up bad. I was wrong to you and I was wrong to the God you have taught me to serve. I am not even worthy to be called your son. Make me one of your hired servants.'"

I left for home first thing in the morning. It took longer to get home than it had to get away. Every step felt like I had 100-pound weights around my ankles, but I kept on walking. Just as my house came into view over the hill, it looked like something was moving toward me on the road. As I got closer and it got closer, I finally recognized what it was. It was my dad. He was running right at me. I couldn't get a good look at his face because he was moving so fast. He was on me before I could figure out his attitude. He grabbed me with what seemed like a bear hug, pinning my arms to my sides. I immediately started in on my speech.

"I messed up; I was lazy and I messed up bad. I was wrong to you and I was wrong to the God you have taught me to serve. I am not even worthy to be called your son . . . ."

Before I could finish, I realized he was crying. And he was kissing me. I just stood there, not even able to finish my speech. He had cut me off anyway and he started yelling to his servants.

"Quick," he said. "Bring the best robe and put it on my son. Put a ring on his finger and put sandals on his feet. Get the calf that's ready to be killed and prepare a banquet. It's time to have a feast and celebrate because this son of mine was as good as dead to me, and now he's alive again; he was lost and now he is found."

My father took me back. He didn't ask any questions. He didn't point any fingers. After all I'd done, he just took me back. Wow.

One of the hardest things the older generation tries to teach the younger generation is the value of hard work. Every generation also seems to believe that the next generation is virtually a lost cause because that younger group doesn't seem to know the value of hard work. Obviously, somewhere along the line, each generation learns that hard work is necessary and being lazy leads nowhere. The story of the prodigal son and his father is one of the bridging of this generational gap. The father received the satisfaction of knowing his son had learned the value of hard work, and the son had the satisfaction of learning that hard work had its benefits. Would you consider yourself lazy? Where do you stand on the issue of the value of hard work?

DO THIS: Evaluate the responsibilities you have. List the responsibilities you have related to home, school, church, work, community activities, etc. After you have listed your responsibilities, check if you think having this responsibility is fair or unfair. Then answer the questions that follow that relate to your evaluation.

Responsibility	Fair	Unfair

If none of your responsibilities seem unfair to you, you either have very few responsibilities or you are doing a good job having your priorities straight. Go on to the next chapter.

If any of your responsibilities seem unfair to you, ask yourself the following questions:

1. Do you feel you have too many responsibilities?
2. Did you volunteer for too many things? If so, you are over-committed and you probably should look at which things you can eliminate.
3. Were these things assigned to you by someone else? If so, did he/she have a right to require this of you? Why did this person choose you to have this responsibility?
4. Is this a responsibility that must be done by you?

5.   If you don't carry out this responsibility, who will?

6.   If this responsibility is neglected, what will happen?

Now that you have evaluated your responsibilities, especially those you feel are unfair, write down your feelings and/or conclusions about these issues.

MEMORY VERSE FOR "LAZY PRODIGAL SON"

Prov. 12:24 Diligent hands will rule, but laziness ends in slave labor. (NIV)

Daring

MIRIAM

Ex. 2:1–9

I will not hesitate to do what has to be done.

Several months ago, a rumor spread like wild fire through our camp. I couldn't believe my ears. It was being said that the midwives, the women who helped deliver the Hebrew babies, had been ordered to kill every boy child born to our mothers. My own mother was due to have my little brother or sister any day now, and all of us were really nervous. How could anybody just kill a cute little newborn baby? I hated Pharoah for making such a wicked law, but I knew anything was possible from a man as evil as he was.

You see, a long time ago, my people the Hebrews were made slaves of the Egyptians. Pharoah, the Egyptian king, forced us to serve them because he was afraid that we'd join forces with his enemies and wipe him out. I wish we had, but it was too late to talk about that now. My people have been slaves for so long that it seems we don't know how to do or be anything else. Pharoah just does whatever he wants to do with us and we can't say a thing.

My parents have hope, though, that our God will deliver us one of these days. After surviving back-breaking hours of work for the Egyptians, Mom and Dad talk of a deliverer—someone God will raise up to get us out of this madness. I want so badly to believe them, but the hardships keep getting in the way of making my faith as strong as theirs. I want the deliverer to hurry and show up. I'd be first in line to help him free us from this terrible slavery. I'd do anything.

One day when I was plotting how my underground spy ring would kidnap the Pharoah and float him down the Nile River with no oars, my daydreaming was suddenly interrupted by my mother's ear-splitting scream. "Miriam, go get the midwife. It's time!"

"But Mom, I can help deliver the baby. I'm big enough. I'm scared of what they might do if you have a boy," I complained.

"Don't worry. Our God will . . . ," she paused and winced through another contraction, " . . . He'll take care of us. Now go, child. It will be soon."

Although I didn't want to, I ran to the house of Shiphrah, the midwife. She was just coming in from another delivery when I got there. I silently wondered what she had done to their baby. "Momma's ready to have the baby," I said with a cold, icy stare. "I told her that I could help her myself, but she insisted that I come get you." I was trying my best to make my implication clear. I didn't trust this woman and I wanted to be sure she knew it.

I didn't know quite how to react when Shiphrah just stared at me for about ten seconds. Then she just picked up her things and said, "Let's go, child. Show me the way."

Momma was in agony when we got to the house. Shiphrah sent me to get more water and clean bed covers. I didn't want to leave her alone with Momma but I had to obey. I got back just in time to hear my little brother make his first sounds. Then Shiphrah surprised me. "I can't believe how healthy you women are," she was saying to Momma as she gave the baby his first bath. "Before I can make it to the house, your babies are born. I can't fool you by saying your boy children are stillborn. You do a great job of hiding those boys too." Then she left.

I jumped up and down and danced all around the room. "She isn't killing the boys. She's lying to the Pharoah." I sang over and over as I jumped and twirled around the room.

"All right Miriam, all right. Settle down. We still have a big problem. You have to help me hide the baby from Pharaoh's taskmasters."

"Anything, Momma, anything."

For the next three months, we did a pretty good job of hiding little Moses, but the bigger he grew and the stronger his lungs became, the harder it was to conceal him. Momma finally came up with a plan that broke our hearts, but it looked like our only solution. We would have to get him out of the main settlement and the only safe route would be the river. Momma made a watertight bassinet with a lid for Moses. The plan was to float him down the river and pray he'd be found by some kindly Egyptian family who would take him in.

There were several glitches to this plan. #1, Moses was getting heavy and the basket might sink with his weight. #2, there were crocodiles in the river who could swallow him for lunch in one gulp. And #3—and this was the worst of all three—the river flowed directly past Pharaoh's palace. If someone there found him—well, tears come to my eyes when I think of what they'd do. We had no other choice if Moses were to have any chance of survival.

All of us, even Daddy, cried and cried the morning we had to let him go. We all got up at 4:30 a.m., while it was still dark. Daddy and Momma kissed and hugged Moses until I thought he'd be soaked through with their tears. I had the job of sneaking Moses, in his little basket, down to the Nile. I finally crept out of the house and walked briskly through the back streets of the settlement, staying as close as I could to the houses and trying not to make Moses cry.

It seemed like it took me forever and I was almost seen twice, but I finally made it to the riverbank. I lifted the basket lid, kissed and hugged my little brother, and looked at him for a long time. I even prayed to Momma's God that He would keep Moses safe and float him to a really nice family.

I finally let the basket start to float. I also had a long stick to help me keep the basket from floating too far out into the river, and to beat off any possible hungry crocs. The current was unusually swift and sometimes I had to jog to keep up with it. I was moving as quietly as I could, but the rustling of the reeds made me nervous as I pushed through. Every time I stepped on one making it break and snap, it sounded to me as loud as the beat of the taskmasters' drums.

I don't know how long I followed the basket because I was concentrating so hard on hiding and keeping it close to the bank. That's why it shocked me when I suddenly heard voices up ahead. Just as I came to a clearing, I saw them. "Oh no, it couldn't be worse," I thought. Pharoah's daughter, the princess herself, was bathing at the river's edge.

Just then, a baby croc nosed itself right between me and the basket. In its effort to sniff the basket's contents, it managed to push it right out into the open. I hit at it with my stick and by the time I reached for Moses, the basket was in the clear. That's when she saw it.

"What have we here?" she questioned. Of necessity, I had learned their language and, although she was an evil Egyptian, her face looked sweet and her voice flowed like honey. This was my first time hearing one of them speak in a kind tone. Still, my heart leaped to my throat and my temples when she fished the basket from the water and lifted the lid.

Moses began to cry. "It's a baby!" one of her maiden exclaimed.

"Oh, he's so cute," cooed another.

"Where'd he come from?"

"Mistress, what will you do with him?"

The princess examined Moses closely as she held and comforted him. I could tell she knew where he had come from. The silence deafened me as I waited for her to reply to her maidens. She held him looking into his smooth, trusting little eyes. Would she plunge him into the river, holding him under until the water pushed life's air from his lungs?

After what seemed like an eternity, she answered quietly and matter-of-factly, "The gods have sent me a son. I will keep him myself and raise him here in the palace." Then she faced the river and proclaimed in a louder voice, "I will need a nurse as perfect for the child as the child is in his face and form."

Was she really petitioning her gods or was this some game to flush me out? Was it a trick? I had to take the chance. I knew what I had to do.

I emerged from my hiding place and, without so much as an explanation as to what I was doing there, I said, "Princess, I know where I can find a nurse for the baby."

She looked at me and I knew she knew.

"Go get the nurse," was all she said.

When it counted, Miriam had to be daring. She had to put it all on the line, take a chance, and leave the results up to God. Little did Miriam know at the time, but she was actually living out her daydreams of helping the deliverer that she heard her parents talk about. When he grew up, her very own brother, Moses, became the deliverer of the Hebrew people. He confronted the Pharaoh and God used him to lead the Hebrew people away from their harsh slavery in Egypt to the Promised Land.

Miriam had watched as the water swept Moses into his destiny when he was an infant. She was there to see Moses deal with water again, years later, as the Red Sea changed from a barrier to a blessed escape route. Again Miriam danced after her people were safely on the other side of the river watching the Egyptian army drown in the Nile.

Sometimes, teenagers seem to make some decisions much too quickly, but maybe your quickness to action could work to your advantage. Because you are not afraid of much, you rush in when adults would be prone to hang back and check things out a lot longer. There is much to be said about patience and wisdom, but sometimes, the right thing to do is to move immediately. The trick is to figure out when to move and when to wait. If you concentrate on God's word and pray for His guidance, you will be ready to move quickly when He needs you to.

DO THIS :   In the following situations, say whether you would do something right away (charge), do nothing (choke), or think it over for some time (check). Explain what you would do and why under the correct column.

SITUATION	CHARGE	CHOKE	CHECK
1. Your best friend announces that he/she is going to commit suicide because life just isn't worth living anymore.			
2. A very close girlfriend (age 16) tells you that she is pregnant. Her parents are very important people in your church. She does not want to make the family ashamed so she has decided to get an abortion.			
3. A popular guy friend is having trouble passing his classes because of the pressure of being the starting forward on your school's cham-			

pionship bas-ketball team. He decides he needs extra help through pills and ste-roids.			

Each of the above situations requires lots of prayer, but none of them can wait for your action. Suicide is always a critical issue. Your friend's parents need to know as soon as possible that the problems have gotten really serious. Even if you don't understand how your friend can possibly be feeling the way he/she does, you must take it seriously that his/her problems are real for him/her. Death is final and there is no turning back if the suicide attempt is successful. If you can't contact the parents, tell a school official or someone at your church. Watch for tell-tale signs that your friend is really serious about the threat. Suicidal people can seem very rational and they calculate exactly how things will be done. They also sometimes begin to give their personal things away. For example, your friend may show up at your house with his whole CD collection and say that it's all now yours. (See Eccl. 9:10 and 1 Pet. 1:17)

An unplanned pregnancy is no less traumatic. The pressure of not wanting to disappoint parents and friends is a heavy weight for many young women. However, abortion always ends up with at least one dead victim, and that's the baby. Sometimes, the proce-dure itself goes bad and your friend could find her own health in danger as well as her future childbearing years. As a minor, your friend is still under the care of her parents and they are ultimately responsible for her and her health. Get her to a responsible, Chris-tian adult before she walks through the doors of an abortion clinic and it is forever too late. (Ex. 20:13)

Finally, there is a real temptation to use drugs that promise to "just help you over this little hump". Even legal drugs and over the counter medications, when taken for the wrong reasons and in the wrong doses, can be very dangerous and very addicting. Remember, no junkie started out saying, "Oh yes, I want to be a junkie when I grow up. I want to risk my life using dirty needles, spend all the money I can earn or steal to snort up my nose, and hang out with undesirable, scary individuals who are probably all wanted by the police." The junkie very possibly started out just like your friend, experimenting with drugs just to get over "this little hump". (See Eph. 5:18)

"What will my friends say," you ask, "when they find out I was the one who sold them out?" Until they come to understand how dangerous their actions could have been, they may not feel very good about you. You may even lose them as friends. However, what's better, to lose a live friend or to attend the funeral of a dead one? Eventually, a real friend will see you as the real friend you are. (See Prov. 17:17)

Memory Verse For "Daring Miriam"

Prov. 28:26 He who trusts in himself is a fool, but he who walks in wisdom is kept safe. (NIV)

Dishonest

JACOB

Gen. 25:21–34, 27, 28:1–10
I will not be honest.

I thought I was so smart. The plan was sweet; it all sounded so simple. However, now that I'm out here in the wilderness by myself, it doesn't seem so great. I hope you've never done something you later regretted. It's not a good feeling. Let me tell you about what happened to me.

Let me start by telling you a little about my family. My grandfather was the great Abraham. God gave him a message telling him that he would be the father of a very special nation of people. These people would be greatly used by God Himself to carry out His plans. Can you imagine how excited he and Grandmother Sarah must have been to hear this about their own children and other future descendants? Well, after some ups and downs and long years of waiting, Granddad and Grandmother finally had their child, my dad Isaac. My dad married my mother, Rebekah, and then we boys came along.

When I say "we boys," I don't just mean several male children. I am a twin. My older brother's name is Esau and we are as different as night and day. He's the athletic, outdoorsy type. You know, he's all buff and he and my dad love to do junk like hunting and fishing. As for me, I'm the brainiac. Okay, you might call me a nerd, but I can think twice as fast as anybody I know and can talk my way in and out of any situation. Mom sort of favors me, I guess because she can understand me better than she can understand Esau. His super macho thing gets pretty tired.

Anyway, before we were born, my parents received a message from God telling them they would have twins and that the younger one would serve the older one. This was totally backward according to our traditions. The oldest male always gets all the play when it comes to the inheritance of the family. So, when we were born, our parents were very interested in our birth order. Although Esau came out first, I was holding on to his heel. It was like I didn't want him to get away or be too far ahead of me. Because of this, my parents named me Jacob, which means "heel holder". When I, the younger brother, grew to be my mother's favorite, she periodically kept me aware of the prophesy, wondering exactly when it was going to kick in.

I saw my chance one day when Esau and I were in our teens. Esau came in hot, tired, and hungry from another one of his hunting trips. I just happened to be making my lunch when he stumbled into the tent.

"Give me some of that soup," he demanded.

He was a pain in the behind and had always gotten his way by bullying me around. I thought about all those times he had made fun of me in front of my friends and how dad was always bragging about all the athletic things he did and I was sick of it. This time, I was determined not to punk out. There had to be a way to make him pay. Then it came to me.

"Sell me your birthright." I braced myself for the explosion that was sure to come out of his mouth. After all, this was a pretty drastic payment request for a bowl of soup, but hey, I had nothing to lose.

Imagine my surprise when all he said was, "Look, I'm getting ready to die of starvation and thirst; what good is my birthright doing me right now?"

I couldn't believe he was really this stupid. "Give me your word, man. You're actually selling me your birthright for this bowl of soup?".

"Yeah, yeah. Now give me the bowl and a spoon."

It was done! I had the birthright of the firstborn. I waited until he had finished eating my lunch and had left to clean his hunting weapons before I ran to tell Mom what had happened. I knew she would be really excited to find out that the prophesy had been fulfilled. But when I told her, although her eyes brightened, she told me something I didn't know before.

"That's good, son, real good. But, in order to rule over your brother, you'll also have to receive the blessing of the firstborn."

I knew what that meant and I hadn't even thought about it until now. You see, when the head of the family is getting ready to die, he calls his kids to him and blesses them. The oldest, like I said before, gets all the play and the father blesses him with all he will need to take over as the family leader. This blessing completed the meaning of the birthright. Mom and I would just have to wait and see what would happen next, but because the birthright thing went so smoothly, I got kind of cocky about how I'd soon have the blessing too.

My chance came sooner than I thought. Dad was getting pretty old and he had gone totally blind several years ago. One day, he called Esau to his bed side.

"Son," he said, "I know that I don't have much longer to live. I want you to go hunting and catch my favorite dinner—venison. Bring it back, cook it and bring it to me so that I can give you the family blessing."

Mom overheard this conversation and as soon as Esau left, she called me.

"Okay Jacob, now's our chance. Your father just told Esau to go hunting so that he can prepare the blessing meal. Here's what I want you to do. Go out to our flock and bring me two goats. I'll fix them like your dad likes. *You* take the meal to your dad. He's blind. You can get the blessing."

"Mom, I never would have thought you could come up with a plan like this. You're pretty sneaky. One problem, though. Esau is hairy, my skin is smooth. I could never pass for him. You know how Dad likes to pat him on the back and hug him. As soon as he touches me, I'll be found out and he'll give me a curse instead of a blessing. It's too risky."

"Boy, if that happens, let the curse be on me. Don't you think I've thought that through? I wasn't born yesterday either."

"Okay," I thought half reluctantly, half expectantly. "I sure hope you know what you're doing."

So, while the meat was cooking, Mom proceeded to trim the skin of the goats and cover my hands, arms, and neck with it so that they would feel hairy if my dad touched me. She then got me one of Esau's robes and told me to put it on. Of course, it was way too big, but I draped it over my own clothes the best I could. As soon as the meal was steaming hot on the plate, I was ready to take it to my father. I was about to see the fulfillment of the prophesy but it wasn't feeling right. Mom noticed I was hesitating and pushed me to get me through the door of Dad's tent.

I greeted him with the traditional greeting for this kind of occasion. "My father," I said.

As soon as I had finished speaking, I knew I was in trouble. He answered, "Here am I; who art thou, my son?"

He recognized my voice! Oh no. Mom and I hadn't even thought about this. My heart jumped into my throat and I barely got the lie out. In a little deeper tone, I tried my best to imitate my brother's voice. "I am Esau your oldest son, Dad. I've done exactly what you asked me to do just a little while ago. Come on, eat your venison so that you can bless me."

"How is it that you found it so quickly?"

This was getting worse and worse by the minute. It would have been so much easier if I didn't have to answer all these questions; if I didn't have to say anything. After all, if I didn't say anything, I wouldn't really be lying, would I? But he asked a question that I had to answer. I had to think fast.

"I hardly had to hunt for it at all. The Lord your God brought it to me."

"Come close to me so that I can feel you, my son, and tell whether you really are Esau or not."

I was caught, I knew it. As I approached my dad, I prepared myself for him to speak a curse on the rest of my life. I was too far into it to turn and run so I went to him.

Dad felt my arms and the back of my neck. "The voice is Jacob's, but the hands are Esau's. Are you sure you're Esau?"

"Dad, yeah. I'm Esau."

He sat back and relaxed. "All right," he said. "Bring me the meal."

It seemed to take him forever to eat that meal. I kept glancing out the tent door, hoping Esau wouldn't show up. When Dad finally finished, he asked me to jump through one more hoop. "Come near now and kiss me, my son." When I did, I could tell that he was smelling my robe. He said, "Yes, your smell is the smell of a field which the Lord has blessed."

He proceeded to give me the Blessing. He pronounced for me the dew of heaven, the fatness of the earth, and plenty of corn and wine. That would have been plenty for me, but he went on. Next, he said that people would serve me, nations would bow down to me, I would be lord over my brother, and all the family now and to come would bow down to me. He ended by saying that everyone who cursed me would be cursed and everyone who blessed me would be blessed.

Wow, I had no idea the Blessing was that deep. I left Dad's tent a little stunned and just in time to see Esau coming over the far hill with his catch. I ducked around back.

Needless to say, when Esau found out that the Blessing had been taken, he was pretty hot. He was so hot that he threatened to kill me as soon as Dad died. Luckily for me, Mom heard him make the threat, warned me, and I got the heck out of there.

Now here I am, alone in the wilderness, on my way to live with an uncle I've never even met. Lots of good the birthright and Blessing are doing me here. I'm seriously beginning to wonder what good it was to do all that lying and conniving.

There is always a negative end to sin. One of the Ten Commandments says, "Don't bear false witness against your neighbor" (Ex. 20:16 KJV). The Bible also says, "These six things doth the LORD hate: yea, seven are an abomination unto him: A proud look, a lying tongue . . . " (Prov. 6:16–17 KJV).

Jacob knew that lying was wrong, but he did it anyhow to get his way. He even fooled himself into thinking he was doing God a favor. After all, how else was God going to have His prophesy fulfilled for him to rule over his brother? Duh. Like God needed Jacob's help (or ours) doing anything.

By the way, here's another trip. Another meaning for Jacob's name is "supplanter". A supplanter is one who takes the place of someone else by force. How true that became, but to the shame of his whole family.[1]

DO THIS:

Do you tell the truth if...?	Who do you tell?	Why do you tell the truth?	How do you say it?
The teacher assumes you have cheated on a test - and you did. She confronts you.			
You saw the person who stole a copy of the English Literature final. Your teacher finds out that the test has been stolen, but doesn't know by whom. He says he must either find out who took the test, or he will write a new, harder exam.			

[1] Read all of the story of Jacob's life found in Genesis, chapters 26–50. You will see how the tricks he played and the lies he told early in his life came back to haunt him.

Dishonest

Do you tell the truth if...?	Who do you tell?	Why do you tell the truth?	How do you say it?
Your little brother saw a drive-by shooting. Your friend, who knows gang members in the guilty gang, tells you that the gang are looking for that little boy so they can keep him quiet. Do you tell the police that your little brother was a witness?			
A department store clerk gives you too much change.			
When Christmas shopping, the person packing your purchases mistakenly puts things in your bag that belong to another customer. You are not charged for these items.			
You see a senior citizen drop a wallet in a crowded mall. When you pick it up, you look in it and realize it contains $500.00 in cash. The wallet contains sufficient identification for you to be able to return it and you see the store into which the person went.			

Do you tell the truth if...?	Who do you tell?	Why do you tell the truth?	How do you say it?
You did not finish your term paper and today is the deadline. However, you know that if you have an excused absence, you can turn work in on the day you return. You decide to stay home from school to finish the paper. The day you return, what do you tell the school secretary your absent excuse is?			

MEMORY VERSE FOR "DISHONEST JACOB"

Prov. 12:22 The Lord detests lying lips, but he delights in men who are truthful. (NIV)

Chapter 8

No Discernment

JOSEPH

Gen. 37
I will not keep my mouth shut.

Hi. My name is Joseph. I'm next to the youngest in a family of thirteen kids. If you count dad, mom, dad's other wife, and his two secondary wives (it's a long story), there are actually 18 of us. You would probably think that with thirteen kids and 4 wives, my dad would have his hands so full that he wouldn't have much individual time with us. Not so in my case. As a matter of fact, Dad spent so much time on me that . . . Well, I think I'd just better tell you the whole story so you can understand it from the beginning.

My dad should have known that showing favoritism among his kids was a big mistake. But I hear that it's really hard to rise above what you've learned at home as your were growing up, and favoritism was what my dad grew up with. Dad was a fraternal twin. He and his brother Esau were as different as night and day. Uncle Esau was a big, buff dude—tight eight—pack abs, a lineman's wide shoulders, a brick wall chest, and thighs the size of tree trunks. A real man's man. His daddy, my grandpa Isaac, loved "his boy". By contrast, my dad, on the other hand, was the business mind. He more preferred to figure out in his head how much could be hunted down on any one day than to do the actual hunting. He was the more spiritually-attuned twin also and Grandma Rebekah loved her some Jacob. (That's my dad's name.)

This favoritism led to a rivalry between dad and his brother that ended with a horrible estrangement that lasted many years. My dad scandalously tricked Uncle Esau out of both his birthright and his blessing. Because of his treachery, my dad had to literally run away from home like he was in a witness protection program or something because Uncle Esau was going to kill him.

Dad's leaving home led to his meeting of my grandmother's brother, Great Uncle Laban, who was a schister in his own right. What goes around comes around, and dad was tricked by Great Uncle Laban into marrying both of his daughters—Rachel, my mom, and Leah, her older sister.

Then the Baby Wars began. Dad really loved my mom and only married Aunt Leah because he was tricked into it. Since Aunt Leah was being dogged out having to have a husband who didn't really love her, God allowed her to have lots of babies. Well, this made my mom quite ticked off, so she sent her handmaiden to marry Dad and have kids for her. When Mom was successful at this, Aunt Leah did the same thing. (It was crazy, I know, but it really did happen that way.)

Finally, after all this drama, Mom got pregnant. Dad couldn't have been happier and that's when that favoritism gene kicked in. I was the son of the favorite wife. Although there were ten sons and one daughter ahead of me, Dad favored me. When I was 17, he even presented the honor coat of the firstborn to me to show that he intended for me to carry on as head of the family line when he passed away.

Dad sensed that I was going to be different. I think God may have told him I'd have some special gifts, but parents have to be careful and wise with knowledge like that. If they handle it wrong, the kid is sure to handle it wrong too.

So, being a spoiled little snot, I couldn't keep my mouth shut or pride to myself. Even if there were something special about me, I didn't have to shake it shamelessly in my brothers' faces like I did. For example, no matter what the weather was like, I wore my honor coat. I was also a snitch. I would tell Dad all the bad stuff my brothers did while they were working away from home. And I admit it, I was clueless because I still had no idea why my brothers rolled their eyes whenever I was around. I shrugged it off but everything I did just caused them to hate me more and more.

Then one night I had this awesome dream. I couldn't wait to tell my brothers.

"Hey you guys," I yelled, "guess what? I had this dream I need to tell you about."

"What are you dreaming about, you tattle-tale?" Gad asked.

"Wait 'til you hear," I answered as I jogged up to where they were eating their lunch. They started to get up to leave, but Reuben, my oldest brother, made them stay.

"Come on, you guys. Let's hear what the runt has to say. This should be good," he mocked.

"Okay," I began. "We were all gathering our sheaves in the field. Each of us had a bundle. All of a sudden, my sheaf stood up straight. Then, all your sheaves gathered around and bowed down to mine."

When I finished telling it, at first they all just looked at me like they were in shock. Then some of them started laughing and some started making fun of me.

"Oh yeah, right," Simeon laughed. "Like we're really going to bow down to you. Please."

"Boy, you'd better go somewhere to have a reality check," sneered Levi. "I'm the last person who plans to bow down to some little spoiled brat."

Naphtali chimed in, "The sad part about it is, he actually thinks his dream means something. Are you going to rule over us? Boy, please. Get out of here."

Well, of course I was disappointed that they didn't give me any props for my dream. I began to think that maybe they were right though. After all, they were all bigger and stronger and they knew a lot more about the world than I did. Then I had another dream that was so real, that I had to tell my family again. This time, I told everybody while my father was around.

"Listen, I had another dream that you all have to hear about."

"Oh no," Simeon broke in. "Here we go again."

"Let my boy talk, Simeon," said Dad. "I'd like to hear what his dream was about."

"Okay," I began. "The sun, the moon, and eleven stars were all bowing down to me . . . "

Dad stopped me. "Joseph, you've gone too far this time. I heard about your other dream in which your brothers' sheaves bowed down to yours. Now you think that I, your mother, and your brothers will actually get to the place where we will bow to the ground before you? You're getting too big for your britches, son."

My dad said what he did just to cool them down. He may have made me stop talking, but I know he listened to what my dreams meant. As I looked around the room though, I saw something evil in my brothers' eyes.

Several days later, my brothers went out to take the flocks to pasture. They would be away for a few days. After a while, my dad sent me to go check on them. He told me to bring a report back to him about how they were doing. It took me a while to find them, because for some reason, they had left Shechem where they usually took the flock. I finally found them at Dothan. What happened next was a nightmare.

"Well, well," said Levi with contempt. "Look out there. Here comes the dreamer."

"Dad has probably sent him to spy on us again. You know he'll tell every little tidbit about what we're doing. I think we ought to just kill him and end our misery."

"Yeah," the others agreed. "There are plenty of us to carry on Dad's family without him."

"No," said Reuben. "Let's not kill the kid. We'll just throw him into one of these pits. That way, if an animal comes to get him, too bad, but we won't be the ones responsible for killing him."

Once I reached where they were sitting, they didn't even let me say hello. They grabbed me, stripped off my honor coat (which I was wearing of course), and threw me into a pit that had been dug to be an animal trap. I screamed, begged, and pleaded all afternoon for them to let me out. I could hear them up there eating their lunch and laughing at me and my dreams. I also heard Reuben tell them he'd run over and check on the flock while the rest of them ate. As soon as he left, Judah had a new idea that he shared with the rest of the brothers.

"It won't do us any good to kill that kid. We'd be guilty of murder, have to cover it up, and there'd be no profit in it for us at all. Look, there are some traders, probably on their way to Egypt. Let's sell him. After all, he is our brother so we really shouldn't kill him."

Remarkably, the others agreed to sell me! While a couple of them got me out of the pit, the others flagged down the traders and made the deal. My struggle and protests were not good. I saw my own brothers take 20 shekels of silver as payment for me. (To give you an idea of how much money that may have been, one shekel equaled about 4 days' wages, so 20 shekels would have been equivalent to 80 days' wages. At minimum wage of $6.00/hour, that would be about $3,840.00.)

Before I knew it, I was in Egypt. Here I was, 17 years old, a slave, away from my family, and surrounded by strange people and a strange language. Me and my big mouth.

Years later, Joseph learned that Reuben actually had his back and had planned to sneak back to get him out of that pit when the others weren't looking. However, his good intentions didn't work. When Reuben returned to get him out of the pit, he panicked and tore his clothes wondering what he was going to tell his dad. He knew his dad would hold him responsible. So, the brothers came up with the bright idea to kill an animal, spread its blood on Joseph's honor coat, and tell their dad that an animal must have attacked and killed him as he was traveling to look for them. Their dad bought the story but mourned for years and years.

Joseph's story turns out okay in the end, but only after he went through much more suffering. He finally got his mouth under control, speaking to take care of his business, honor God, and interpret dreams. He ended up second in command of all of Egypt.

Because Joseph was not able to discern when to talk and when to be quiet, his brothers hated him. Like Joseph, other teenagers tend to get into most of their trouble because of their mouths. Either they brag about something and then feel obligated to prove it, or they speak before thinking, someone hears them, and then it's "on". With a little forethought, Christian teens are able to control their tongues, speaking what's appropriate at the right time.

DO THIS :   In the following situations, write down a common response people give before thinking, then write down a more appropriate response that would be fit the situation and glorify God.

Situation	Common/Rushed Response	Appropriate Response
In a classroom, a teacher falsely accuses you of talking or cheating and gives you a punishment.		
At the park, some guys start playing a half-court basketball game while you and your friends were already on the court playing full court.		
The police pull you over and you know you haven't done anything.		
Your parents tell you that you can't go to a school dance or party. You haven't done anything wrong and you realize that they are in a bad mood.		

MEMORY VERSE FOR "NO DISCERNMENT JOSEPH"

1 Pet. 3:10 For, "Whoever would love life and see good days must keep his tongue from evil and his lips from deceitful speech. (NIV)

Chapter 9

Impressionable

RUTH

The Book of Ruth
I will not take the easy way out.

My name is Ruth and my story is a love story. You know how important love is to us teens. Well, I fell in love with this guy who wasn't even supposed to be talking to me. Funny how that always seems to happen.

Anyway, I met Chilion when his family moved to town. Normally a new family in town wouldn't raise that much suspicion, but everyone paid attention to this family. I lived in Moab and they were from Israel. The Israelites were forbidden by their religion to marry anybody who wasn't one of them so they basically had nothing to do with us at all to be sure no one would hook up. This had made them kind of stuck up whenever they came around us. They really thought they were better than us. We had pretty much learned to ignore them and there was a subtle racism-thing happening between us. So you can imagine how everybody in town knew that a family of "them" had moved in down the street.

The new family consisted of the dad whose name was Elimelech, the mom, Naomi, and two sons, Mahlon and Chilion. While the adults gossiped about why they had moved in, we kids went snooping around. My girlfriend Orpah and I didn't care why they had moved in once we got a look at those guys. They were cute! We watched them for about a week trying to get their routine down. They would work with their dad most of the day and run errands to and from the market place and the fields. Every afternoon, their whole family would gather together and Elimelech would talk very seriously and in very low tones to all of them. They would bow their heads at the end of each of these talks, then they'd have their evening meal. After seven days had passed, Orpah and I were ready to burst.

Orpah brought it up first. "Ruth," she said, "I can't stand it any longer. We have to talk to them. They are so cute."

"Orpah, you are so crazy. We can't talk to them," I reminded her. "They hate us just because we're Moabites. They probably think we're going to eat them or something."

"Ruth, don't be ridiculous. Look at them. They're just guys— really cute guys. We just have to get to know them."

"They are cute, but besides that, there's something really different about them. Even watching them for this short time, can't you tell that they aren't like any of the other boys we know? You think it has something to do with their weird religion?"

"I don't care what their religion is. I just want to get to know them."

Our chance came sooner than we thought. We were in the market place picking out fruit when they showed up. Imagine how we felt when they came over and started talking to us.

"Hi, my name's Chilion." The one with the curly brown hair looked directly into my eyes as he spoke. He had rich brown skin and muscles under every inch of it. When he introduced his brother Mahlon, Orpah couldn't take her eyes off of him.

For the next few weeks, whenever we had the opportunity, we would secretly arrange to meet the brothers in the orchard. Our parents on neither side would have approved of our getting together. They were always telling us that we were naive and impressionable and we'd fall for anything. However, the more we got to know Chilion and Mahlon, the more comfortable we felt with them. They were really polite, yet they weren't nerds. They never tried to take advantage of us either. (What a difference from the Moabite guys we knew.) We would take walks and listen as the brothers told us about Israel, their lives back home, and their religion. We found out that they had moved away from their homeland because of a terrible famine. Elimelech was just trying to find someplace that had work for him and food for his family. The land of Moab just happened to fill his needs.

I found myself thinking, "I'm really glad there's no water in Israel." Why was I thinking that way? You guessed it. I knew I was falling in love with Chilion. I soon found out that Orpah loved Mahlon and to our surprise, the brothers were falling in love with us too.

Although Elimelech and Naomi didn't like it, they accepted their sons' announcement that they had fallen in love with these two Moabite girls and intended to marry them. Naomi sat us down and talked to us about how important it was in their religion that we would stop worshipping the gods we were used to praying to and accept their God. It was a little hard to get used to the idea of having only one God, but my love for Chilion helped me. Because I was so accepted by these beautiful people, I found it easier an easier to accept their God.

My parents figured I had lost my mind. All they had ever known was prejudice from any Israelite. Yet, because I was so insistent, my parents said they would meet these Israelites.

Just as I hoped, the charm, grace, and dignity of Elimelech and Naomi won over the suspicions of my parents and, to my great joy, they gave permission for me to be married.

I was barely fifteen when I became Chilion's wife. Orpah married Mahlon a week later. We moved in with our husbands and began to help Naomi keep house. These were the happiest days my life had ever seen, but my happiness was very short lived. My new father-in-law, Elimelech, got sick and was dead within the week. This hit Naomi hard. I had grown to love Naomi as my own mother and I was very concerned about her. It was very difficult for her to make it through the first two weeks after Elimelech's death. She kept a veil over her face and hardly left the house.

Orpah's and my concern quickly moved away from Naomi, though, when Chilion and Mahlon both came down with the same illness that had killed their father. We looked after them day and night, night and day. I worried about Chilion. I loved him so much. I prayed and prayed to the God Chilion had told me so much about. It was no use. Both Chilion and Mahlon died.

So there we were. Naomi was a widow and now had buried both of her only children. To make it even worse, she felt responsible for us, her two young daughters-in-law. Two weeks after Chilion and Mahlon died, Naomi called Orpah and me to sit with her on the porch of the house.

"Ruth and Orpah," she began. "May the Lord be as kind to you as you two have been to me. You are wonderful daughters and I love you. But I have made a decision. God has allowed some terrible things to happen to me. Maybe it's because I'm away from the land He has blessed. I don't know. All I know is that I have decided that I have to go back to Israel, to the area of Judah where I'm from, to my own home town of Bethlehem. I just have to be with my own people again. You girls go on home to your families, I will not hold you responsible for a sad, old woman.

This was a no-brainer. "There's no way I'm leaving you, Naomi," I countered. Orpah agreed with her words, but her eyes betrayed the fact that she wasn't so sure about leaving Moab.

"No," Naomi argued. "Are there any more sons left in me for you? Even if I did marry again and have two more sons, would you wait for them to grow up and then marry them? No, my daughters, return to your homes and start anew."

That's all Orpah needed. Although she would miss Naomi, she kissed her through her tears and went to her room to pack her things.

"Forget it, Naomi," I said. "You are my family now. I promised Chilion that I would become part of his family. If I go back to my home, I would also be leaving the new God that I am getting to know better and better every day. Your God is who I would be leaving if I leave you. I love both you and Him too much to ever turn back."

There was nothing Naomi could say to change my mind. When I started to pack, I was packing to move with Naomi to the city of Bethlehem. I was still young and had no idea what living in this strange new land would be like. Would they accept me as readily as Naomi had? Would I become an old maid? I didn't care. I just wanted to be with the people whom God—the God who was now my God—had chosen.

Like Ruth's family had always said, Ruth was a very impressionable teen. The neat thing about Ruth is that she was impressed with God. It may not be such a bad thing to be labeled "impressionable" if you are "impressed" with who God is, to the point of changing your entire life to line up with what He expects of you. Like Ruth, God expects you to be able to reach past prejudicial attitudes and be impressed with the truth. Try it. The truth is very impressive!

DO THIS: Read these excerpts from the Bible about the following people and write down an impressive
quality you notice.

Job in Job, chapter 1:

_____
_____
_____
_____

Daniel in Daniel, chapter 6:

_____
_____
_____
_____

Mary in Luke 10:38-42 :

_____
_____
_____
_____

Choose one of the above impressive qualities that you would like to
have God help you to develop in your own Christian life. Write
here what that quality is:

_____

Why did you choose that quality?

_____
_____

Find two other Scripture verses to support the fact that this is a
quality that God would want you to have as part of your Christian
life. (You may need to ask a Christian friend or mentor to help you
with this one.)

1. _____
2. _____

Impressionable

Write a short prayer asking God to build that quality into your life.

_____
_____
_____
_____

For continued growth, choose the other qualities one by one and do the same exercise as outlined above.

MEMORY VERSE FOR "IMPRESSIONABLE RUTH"

Ps. 119:33 Teach me, O LORD, to follow your decrees; then I will keep them to the end. (NIV)

Chapter 10

Stubborn

DANIEL

Dan. 1:1–21
I will not eat the king's meat.

Have you ever noticed how you can hang around with your friends day after day and it seems like nothing exciting is ever going happen, then all of a sudden, something or someone jumps into the mix and changes everything? That's just what happened to my boys and me. My name's Daniel. One day, we were just chillin', minding our own business; the next day our whole lives were changed. It happened something like this:

"Man, I can't believe this," Mishael exclaimed. "Things just weren't supposed to happen this way. Man, I had plans for my future, plans for my education, plans for . . . "

Hananiah had heard enough. "Shut-up, man. Quit whining like a little girl. There's nothing you can do about it, so just relax."

"Look dude," Mishael shot back, "the last thing I am is some little girl. And I have every right to complain about some foreigner busting in here and just snatching our lives away from us like they own us."

"I know, man," Azariah agreed. "This is whack!"

I was the fourth Muskateer of our group, and I had been just chillin' in the corner through the whole conversation. Anybody who knows me knows I'm always ready with a reality check. "Truth is, Dawgs," I said, "they **do** own us."

The awkward silence proved I had turned them out again. Finally, Mishael spoke up.

"You sure know how to take the fire out of a brother. You just got it like that. But still man, I'm through. This is messed up. We don't know anything about Babylon. We're Jews, not stinking Babylonians. How are they going to just come in here and take us over and then expect us to just lie down and take it?" Mishael's anger was quickly welling up again.

"Look," Azariah broke in trying to diffuse the situation. "There was nothing we could do. Our little Israelite army was no match for the Babylonian machine. We're lucky they didn't just come in here and kill all of us. After all, that's what God told our ancestors to do when we first came in to take over the Promised Land. I'm sure the Babylonians knew our history. Even though the situation is messed up, I'd rather be alive than dead.

Hananiah now joined in. "I know, man. So it's no use whining, like I said before. The way I see it, we're making out pretty good. Just because our parents are high up in the government, we are considered "the chosen few" We won't be kickin' it like the rest of the folks they've conquered. We'll be living large in the king's palace.

Azariah shot back, "Yeah man. Good thing we listened to teacher's pet Daniel over there and kept up with our work in school. Remember how he was always sweating us . . . "

"I was not sweating you man," I protested.

"Yes you were dude," Azariah continued. "You were always sweating us about getting a study group together and doing the papers on time and turning in all of the homework. I was eaves-dropping on my parents the other night and they were talking about who got chosen and who didn't. Seems like that King Neb, uh, Nebu . . . "

"That's Nebuchadnezzar, fool. What did you hear?" Hananiah asked impatiently.

"Whatever," Azariah said as he smacked Hananiah in the back of the head. "Anyway, seems like their king wanted only the smartest of our Israelite nobility for whatever he has in mind."

Mishael couldn't hold his pride in any longer. "Yeah Dawg, that does take a little of the sting out of this whole capture thing. It really doesn't sound so bad to hang out at the palace. I also heard that they didn't only want the smartest, they also wanted the most handsome ones of us. On that point, it's clear why they picked me."

We threw everything we could find at Mishael as he threw his arms up to shield that mug he was so proud of.

Despite this joking around, by the looks they gave me, I could tell that my face was telling the true story of my discomfort. "I don't care how good it looks, there's got to be a catch. They can't just want us to kick back in their palace. They've got their own young guys with brains and looks. Something's up. My dad always says, 'If it looks too good to be true, it probably is.' They want something from us. I haven't quite figured it out yet, but I'm going in there with my eyes open, looking for the catch."

A few days later, the Babylonian guards came to gather us, along with the other chosen young men of Israel, arrange us into a caravan, and move us out. Azariah, Mishael, and Hananiah and I were indeed among a large group of the best and the brightest of Israel's royal families and nobility embarking upon a journey that would take us from our homeland to the Babylonian capital. Although our captors were trying to keep the atmosphere relaxed, we couldn't help but notice that our escorts were armed and their faces, though pleasant, made it clear that they had no intention of losing anyone along the way.

Once the caravan arrived at the Babylonian capital, we were assigned rooms along the courtyard on the palace grounds. I have to admit that we were impressed by what we saw as we passed by

the rooms that surrounded the palace garden. There were steaming baths, a massage area, an exercise/fitness/weight room, and many
secluded gazebos where you could enjoy uninterrupted reading
and study time.

We were also assigned officials who would be in charge of us.
They would assign us our schedules, show us around, etc. We were
all given several days to get used the place and then there would be
a meeting. It was at the meeting that my fears were realized.

"Come on in quickly," ordered the official at the front of the
room. We filed in, speaking in whispers to one another, as we found
our seats along the rows of benches behind long tables. The official
spoke through an interpreter. The Babylonian language sounded
strange to our Jewish ears and the interpreter sounded even
stranger, speaking Hebrew with a heavy Babylonian accent. "On
the table in front of you, you will find papyrus and a writing in-
strument. Take notes. Everything that is said to you from this day
forward is for you to learn and remember."

I shot a look toward Hananiah and mouthed the words, "Here
it comes."

The official continued, "The first things we're going to deal with
are your names."

"Our names?" questioned Mishael. "What's wrong with our
names?" The official glared in our direction as the interpreter
quickly told him what the outburst meant.

"Well, well," intoned the official through the interpreter as he
stepped away from the podium and approached the place where
Mishael was seated, "an outspoken one. Do you have something
to say to me about your name?" The man glared at Mishael, caus-
ing him to lose some of his nerve. Just as he was about to sit down,
I couldn't help having his back.

"Yes sir, we do." All eyes shifted from Mishael to me. I stood up
and, in a very respectful, yet determined tone, continued to make
my point to the official. "Our names are very important to us. My
name is Daniel and it means judge of God. My friend here, Azariah's
name means Jah has helped. Jah is another way we say the name of
our God. Hananiah there has a name that means Jah has favored;

84

and Mishael's name means who (is) what God (is). So you see, each time we say our names, we are reminded of the God of Israel.

"Well, this God you speak of certainly didn't help you against our invasion," retorted the official. He had significantly raised his voice. "Now sit down and listen, and from now on, in this room, you only speak when you are directly spoken to first." The official then returned to the podium. "Gentlemen, you are not in Israel any more. This is Babylon and everything done here is done the Babylonian way. You will learn our language and our ways. You will talk like us, walk like us, dress like us, live like us. You will find that the Babylonian way is the best and, eventually, you will learn to enjoy our way of life. Babylon has swallowed Israel.

My eyes narrowed as I continued to listen.

"Back to my point on our first move. About your names. Those names of yours recognize a god we Babylonians don't know nor do we heed. We honor our king and you will too. Therefore, you can no longer be known by names that speak of Him. And since you four brought yourselves to my attention, you will be first to receive your new names.

"Daniel, you shall now be known as Belteshazzar. Since you're so outspoken and seem to be a leader type, this name speaks of being the keeper of the hidden treasures of Bel, one of our gods. Hananiah, shall be known as Shadrach which reminds us of the inspiration of the sun which we worship. Mishael is now Meshach in honor of our goddess Shach, and Azariah is Abednego whose name now turns our attention to the shining fire which we also worship. You were so attached to names the speak of deity, there you have them."

The official turned his attention to the other young men to assign to them their new names. "They'll never make me forget," I vowed silently.

After all the names were assigned, the official had one more thing to announce and explain for the morning. "You will now learn why we Babylonians are so superior to all our enemies. It's in our incredible diet. You will report to your guide who will inform you of your daily food regimen. You must receive the nutrition of the king's table in order to be strong enough to carry out the tasks we have planned for you. You will not be disappointed.

Once back at our quarters, my friends and I huddled together to whisper our discontent. "I told you there was a catch."

"Yeah man," said Mishael through clenched teeth. "How can they expect me to just give up my name. That's who I am; it's who I've always been. I know I'm pretty, man, but they can't just name me after some goddess chick."

"And I'm no shining fire," added Azariah, "and Hananiah sure as heck ain't no sun."

"And that's the point; that's the catch. Don't you see?" I was intently trying to get my friends to understand. "They take us from our 'hood, change our names, change our diet, and put us through their education. This is nothing but a brain-washing factory. We're supposed to *become* Babylonians. Once we are sucked in by all the best they have to give us, they expect that we'll voluntarily convince the rest of our people to chill out and not give them any problems."

"We become their flunkies," Azariah said as he was pacing the floor, pounding his right fist into the palm of his left hand. "Get the young men from backgrounds who were already being groomed for leadership positions . . . "

"Right," I continued. "Get those who others already knew would one day be telling them what to do. Once we go to our own people, proclaiming the wonders of Babylon, no one will ever want to go back to their humble little lives as Hebrews. They will have literally swallowed us up."

"But man, what are we supposed to do? We have to live and we have to eat," questioned Hananiah.

"We may have to eat," I said, "but we don't have to eat what they give us. Besides, what they want us to eat has probably been offered to their gods and I'm sure it's prepared against our religious laws."

Mishael wanted to do anything that could get back at the Babylonians. "We're down with you, dude. What do you want us to do?"

Stubborn

I had a plan. "We're going to refuse to eat the king's diet. We'll be straight up with them. They are sure to call us crazy and stubborn, but I really couldn't care less. Eating their food makes us break the laws of our God and we're not going to do it. We'll ask them to give us ten days just eating vegetables while all the rest of these guys go ahead and eat what they give them. After ten days, test us to see if we're as strong as the rest. We're still God's people and this may be a small way to show it, but God is going to prove to the Babylonians who He is.

The end of the book of Daniel, Daniel 1:15–20, tells the outcome of this stubborn decision:

> At the end of the ten days they looked healthier and better nourished than any of the young men who ate the royal food. So the guard took away their choice food and the wine they were to drink and gave them vegetables instead. To these four young men God gave knowledge and understanding of all kinds of literature and learning. And Daniel could understand visions and dreams of all kinds. At the end of the time set by the king to bring them in, the chief official presented them to Nebuchadnezzar. The king talked with them, and he found none equal to Daniel, Hananiah, Mishael and Azariah; so they entered the king's service. In every matter of wisdom and understanding about which the king questioned them, he found them ten times better than all the magicians and enchanters in his whole kingdom. (NIV)

Stubbornness may be a characteristic of being a teenager, but in Daniel and his friend's case, their stubbornness was used to stick with what God had taught them. At first they looked strange and their decisions seemed ridiculous, but in the end, they made out better than everyone else around them.

Stubbornly sticking to what God expects will probably make you look strange to people around you. Your decision may be judged as ridiculous. Do you have enough guts to apply God's word to the every day happenings of your life?

DO THIS: You are Care Bear, a Christian teen advise columnist. People have written the following letters to you. Your correspondents want to be stubborn and do things God's way, but they are finding it hard. Write response letters to these young people giving them Godly advise and Scripture on which to base their next move.

Dear Care Bear: My friend Sherry and I are excited about being chosen to the varsity cheerleading squad at our Christian high school. Our squad wants to enter a national cheerleading competition this year that will include both private and public high schools. The problem is, when practice began, we found out that we were being asked to perform sexually suggestive moves. We want to stay on the squad. What should we do? Signed, Cheerleaders for Christ

_____
_____
_____

Dear Care Bear: My boys and I are all of the same nationality. It's common to look negatively at people from other races. The guys like to joke about those women's bodies and those men's looks and personality. I admit I laugh at the jokes, but I'm beginning to feel that those kinds of jokes wouldn't be funny to the people we're talking about and I wouldn't want anybody saying those things about me. My buddies don't know it, but I've even made a friend who is a member of one of the races we joke about. What should I do? Signed Prejudice Free

_____
_____
_____

Dear Care Bear: I like church and I've gone all my life. Now I've started playing YMCA football and the games are on Sunday mornings. My parents are tripping because I want to participate in football. I'll just have to miss church for this season. Help me out. Signed Church Kid

---

Memory Verse For "Stubborn Daniel"

Rom. 12:2 Do not conform any longer to the pattern of this world, but be transformed by the renewing of your mind. Then you will be able to test and approve what God's will is—his good, pleasing and perfect will. (NIV)

Chapter 11

Disrespectful

SHADRACH, MESHACH, AND ABEDNEGO

Dan., Chapter 3
We will not respect man's laws over God's laws.

You have probably heard about us because of our more famous friend, Daniel. We were with Daniel when we were captured by the Babylonians. We were down with him when he refused to eat the king's meat. We all went on a vegetarian diet and ended up being smarter and stronger than everybody else who had been captured with us. Well, time has passed. We're still here in Babylon, but now we're officials under King Nebuchadnezzar. You may be wondering how we as Jews managed to ease our way into such important jobs. Believe it or not, it all happened because we *disrespected* the king. I'm Meshach, and since I was the first one to catch a hint of what was up, let me take you back and let you know how it went down.

Shadrach and Abednego arrived at my office at the same time, smiling, giving dap, and hugging with that brother-hug good friends use. "It's been too long, dudes," announced Abednego. "The Babs are keeping us busy. How have you been, dawgs?"

Shadrach answered, "Man, the Babs are all over me too. I really can't complain that much. My job is cool, the apartment's nice, but it's still not home."

"It's been three years since the Neb captured us." I reminisced as I stared out of my second story office window. "Funny, but I still miss home too, man. No matter how hard they have tried, they haven't been able to make Babylonians out of us, have they?"

Abednego was ready with a comeback, "No way, man. That's why, at least behind their backs, I call them Babs and that's why you call King Nebuchadnezzar, the Neb. They don't even deserve the courtesy of having us say their whole names. They thought they had us when they changed our names, but they had to shut-up when God showed Himself to them through our vegetable diet."

"Yeah man, do you remember the looks on their faces when Daniel told them to test us with that diet and then we turned out stronger and smarter than everybody else? That was priceless!" I could tell I had brought back a pleasant memory and we all had a good laugh. Then my expression had to darken. "But you know, the Babs have been on my case ever since I was assigned to this job. They have been trying everything to get me thrown out of here."

"That happens to me too, man," Shadrach returned. "They are so jealous that the Neb has placed Jews over the province. The guys I work with are looking for a way to get me fired too."

Abednego added, "I know Belteshazzer is having the same problem."

I had to correct my brother quickly. "Man, you know Daniel would beat you down if he heard you using that name to refer to him. We got pretty used to the new name thing, but Daniel never did. I'm sure he's fighting his own fights. That's why we don't see him around much any more. They want to be sure he doesn't influence us to rebel even more. Anyway, we have our own problem jumpin'."

Shadrach questioned, "What's up, Dawg?"

"You had better sit down, brothers. We're really in deep this time. I just heard that the Neb got the bright idea of making an image of gold. The thing is nine feet tall and he's setting it up on the plain of Dura."

"Big deal," Abednego shrugged. "We've ignored their stupid idols all this time and they basically haven't sweated us. We'll just ignore this one too."

"Not happening dude," I continued. "This time there's going to be a big dedication service. They've actually made it a vacation day so that everybody can be outside along a sort of parade route when he rides the thing through the city on the way to set it up."

"Again, so what?" said Abednego. "I'm not upset yet. You're making this out to be some big deal and I'm just not feeling you."

"I know you didn't call us all the way up here to tell us some little jive junk like that." Shadrach joined in. "Come out with it. What kind of trouble are we in?"

"Thanks for feeling me, Dawg," I replied. "Look man, it's a set-up. Everybody has to be out at the dedication. Everybody. That includes us. And here's the hitch. Everybody is supposed to bow down to the image as it passes by. The decree has been given that whomever doesn't bow will be thrown into the furnace."

"What? Aw, it's clear now, Dawg," exclaimed Shadrach shaking his head and getting up to pace the floor. "They know we won't bow to an idol. They don't only plan to get us thrown out of our jobs, they plan to get us killed. What are we going to do?"

"I know what we're *not* going to do," answered Abednego. "We're not going to bow to that image. We've hung with God too long to dis Him like this. You down, man?

Abednego reached out his hand, palm down. Shadrach placed his hand on Abednego's and I placed mine on top. We were in this together no matter what.

A few days later was the day of the dedication. Shadrach, Abednego and I filed out to the parade route with all the other workers. As the huge image of gold passed, all kinds of beautiful music played. The decree to bow to the image had been well publicized and people of every nationality bowed reverently as the image processed slowly down the street. The Neb must have been elated. He and his gods were getting all the play.

But as the image passed by us, we stood tall, looking straight ahead. It seemed as though no one even saw that we were standing up because everybody around us was whipped and bent over. But no such luck. Not an hour had passed after we returned to our jobs before we were all summoned to the king's throne room. In essence, we were arrested.

King Nebuchadnezzar was in a rage. "Is it true? Is what I've heard true? After all I've done for you boys, you dishonor me by not bowing to my golden image? I tell you what. You get yourselves ready and I'll give you another chance. Now, when you hear the theme music, you fall down on your knees, your faces, whatever, and worship the image I've made. Then everything will be just fine. But, if you don't bow down, don't expect any special treatment. You will receive the punishment I promised and be tossed into the burning furnace immediately. Don't play me. What god exists who can save you from my hand once I order your frying?"

We didn't even miss a beat to answer the king. Of course, I spoke up first, "O Nebuchadnezzar, we don't even need to discuss this issue. You know where we stand—and my emphasis is on 'stand'—when it comes to your idols and our God."

Abednego joined in, "To answer your question, O King, if you decide to throw us into the blazing furnace, the God that we serve is able to save us from both your furnace and from your hand."

Shadrach continued, "But even if our God decides not to deliver us from this punishment, we want you to know, O King, that we refuse to serve your gods and there's no way we'll ever worship the image of gold you've made."

"You ingrates," Nebuchadnezzar shouted. "Guards, heat the oven seven times hotter than usual. Get my strongest soldiers, tie up these three, and throw them into the furnace now!"

So we didn't even get a chance to say goodbye to any of our friends. The king was so adamant about getting us into the furnace that we weren't even allowed to take off our robes and turbans as most condemned prisoners did. With our hearts beating almost loudly enough to be heard across the room, we were securely tied up and hustled toward the furnace. I was so scared I was ready to wet on myself. We could feel the heat as we got closer and closer to the furnace. As the soldiers shoved us in, the intense heat of the flames killed them! We all tensed up and closed our eyes, expecting to feel our skin start to fry.

After about 10 seconds, we realized nothing was happening. We could still hear the fire fiercely crackling all around us, but it wasn't hot. We were in the middle of a blazing fire and we felt nothing at all. Shadrach figured we had died and were having some sort of out-of-body experience, but it was true. The three of us were standing there in the fire and not being burned. Then we noticed that the ropes that had held us so tightly were gone. Then the biggest surprise of all happened, there was another guy in there with us. He introduced Himself as God's own Son.

Then we started laughing. We just started bustin' up. We couldn't help ourselves. God had taken the heat and destruction out of fire! Incredible. We have no idea how long we were in there with God's Son, but we didn't care. We laughed and talked with Him while we walked around in that fire praising God. You talk about a praise and worship service! We had one in that furnace that afternoon.

Well, while all this was going on inside the furnace, outside the king couldn't erase how he really felt about us. We had been his boys, his special picks. We had proven to be a definite asset to his management team. He actually hated to lose us, but he simply could not tolerate our disrespect of his decrees. I could actually understand his position. He was the king. If we got away with dissing him, others he had conquered would think they could defy his orders too. But as he gazed into the flames of the furnace through his private window, he got the shock of his life.

"Didn't we tie up and throw three men into the fire?" The king was amazed. "Why do I see four men walking around loose? And who is that fourth man? He looks like a son of the gods!"

Nebuchadnezzar approached the furnace door and shouted in, "Shadrach. Meshach. Abednego." Once you actually have an encounter with the Son of God, I guess it doesn't take long to change your tune, no matter who you are, a servant or a king. He said, "I see you are truly servants of the Most High God. Come out of the furnace and come here."

I noticed the king's attitude change immediately. As we exited the furnace, I elbowed my partners. "Did you hear that dawgs? He called us 'servants of the Most High God'. Old Neb is acknowledging the God of Israel. God is all right!" I looked past them to thank the Son of God, but He was gone, just as quickly as He had shown up.

The other two couldn't hold back their grins either as we walked back into the king's throne room. It was so quiet you could hear a pin drop. Those who had dropped a dime on us and gotten us arrested in the first place were just staring with their mouths open as we passed.

"Look at that," one of the governors whispered. "The fire didn't harm their bodies at all. Their robes are not scorched, their hair is not singed, dang, they don't even smell like smoke. Are they magicians of some kind? What the heck is going on?"

Then Nebuchadnezzar said, "Praise be to the God of Shadrach, Meshach and Abednego, who has sent his angel and rescued his servants! They trusted in him and defied the king's command and were willing to give up their lives rather than serve or worship any god except their own God. Therefore I decree that the people of any nation or language who say anything against the God of Shadrach, Meshach and Abednego be cut into pieces and their houses be turned into piles of rubble, for no other god can save in this way" (Dan. 3:28–30).

Then, to the dismay of the government officials who had tired to get us killed, the king promoted us to even higher positions.

If Shadrach, Meshach and Abednego were 15 or 16-years-old when they were taken captive by the Babylonians, by the time of this fiery furnace incident, they would have been older teens of about 18 or 19. They had remained in King Nebuchadnezzar's "chosen child" program, yet had remained faithful to their God. They had made up their minds to respect God's laws even if it meant disrespecting man's laws, so even the threat of death did not deter them. Shadrach, Meshach and Abednego knew the consequences of breaking man's law and were willing to face those consequences.

Disrespectful

DO THIS: Consider the laws in your country, state, city, or school. Are there any laws you can think of that require you to contradict the law of God if you obey the law man has made? Consider the following situations. Write what God's word says about each issue and then write what your response should be. Add other laws you hear of that sound like they will require you to break God's laws.

Man's Law	God's Law	My Response
School Law 1. You cannot pray in school. Consequence? You will be expelled.		
State Law 2. Abortion is okay and permitted for underage girls without parental knowledge or consent.		
City Law 3. Parents are not permitted to spank (physically punish) their children.		
4.		
5.		

MEMORY VERSE FOR "DISRESPECTFUL SHADRACH, MESHACH, AND ABEDNEGO"

Acts 5:29 Peter and the other apostles replied: "We must obey God rather than men! (NIV)

Undisciplined

FIVE FOOLISH GIRLS

Matt. 25: 1–3
We will not prepare for the future.

W̲e were known as the Posse. There were ten of us who grew up in the same neighborhood, went to the same schools, and knew the same people. Now that we were all in high school, the demands of classes meant we had less times to hang out, but we still found some time to see each other, exchange stories, and catch up on the latest news.

So we were really excited when we were all asked to be bridesmaids for Susan's wedding. (Susan is Jael's older sister and Jael is one of the Posse.) Little did we know that this occasion would lead to our little Posse splitting up over the learning of a valuable lesson. But, in order for you to understand what we learned, you first have to know a little bit about Jewish relationships and weddings, so let me tell you the whole story.

Susan was marrying Thaddeus. They made a really cute couple too. Both of them had dark, wavy hair; Susan's reached to her waist and Thad's cut was accompanied by a handsome mustache and full beard. His olive skin tone was about two shades darker than hers because he worked on his family's sheep ranch and was out-of-doors in the blazing sun most days. His coal black eyes had danced and sparkled when they first saw Susan across the room at a Bar Mitzvah. He was simply mesmerized by the flutter of her long eyelashes and her feminine smile and walk. She was only 15, but she already knew how to carry herself as a lady.

Over the next few months, Thaddeus positioned himself to get to know her family and friends, but especially her father. If Thad was really interested, he'd have to approach her dad and ask him if he could marry her, offering some gift to show how much he valued her.

Every time the Posse got together, Jael kept us up to date on the progress of this relationship. We were all very eager to hear about each new development as we hoped and dreamt of this same kind of romance happening to us some day. I vividly recall the day of their formal engagement. Jael gathered us all at our favorite hangout picnic table at the park.

"It was incredibly romantic," Jael exclaimed. She had a habit of talking fast and with her hands, so we really had to listen and watch carefully go keep up with the story.

"He arrived with gifts for everyone in the family. Thad presented Mother with a necklace made of seashells and precious stones. He then gave brother John a fine baby donkey and he presented me with this silver bracelet."

After we gave our appropriate oohs and aahs, she continued.

"He turned from me to Susan, and stood there, just staring at her as if he were in some sort of trance. His love for her is so apparent, he can hardly control himself whenever he sees her. The tenderness just oozed out of his eyes. Anyway, he walked slowly over to her and handed her the most beautiful robe I'd ever seen. It's scarlet with gold threads woven through it—oh, you've just got to see it! He also gave her two gold bracelets and a gold necklace with a pearl charm."

We were mesmerized by the story. This was incredible.

"Then came the crucial gifts. Thad asked my Father if he could marry Susan and then presented him with seven, one-year-old spotless sheep, a ram, a donkey, and a beautifully woven robe."

"My goodness," I shouted. "That boy is serious and seriously rich!"

"What did your father say, Jael?" Simone asked.

"What could he say?" Jael responded. "Father hadn't seen these many riches in his own courtyard in his whole life. Plus, Father really likes Thad and knows that Thad loves Susan. I suppose it's hard for any father to give his daughter to a man . . . "

"But," I interjected, "all those gifts sure took some of the sting out of it!"

Everybody nearly fell off of the picnic bench laughing.

Jael finally got our attention again. "Listen, you guys haven't heard the best part. Susan wants all of us to be her bridesmaids!"

Well, this was almost more than we could stand. The whole Posse started talking excitedly at once. Preparations had to be made. We had only 5 short months to get ready.

And those months whizzed by. I was a lot more excited about getting the new clothes and the special lamp than I was about carrying out the traditions of the ceremony. Half of the Posse was just like me. Simone, Rachel, Orpah, Nila, and I spent most of those months talking about Susan's upcoming wedding, bragging about being in it, and fantasizing about what our own weddings would be like.

On the other hand, Jael, Carmen, Deborah, Liz, and Rita were really serious about their part in the wedding. Susan's and Jael's mom would try to explain to us the importance of our role the day of the wedding. She told us something about how the wedding night had some sort of significance related to the coming of the Messiah. The special lamps we carried were used to represent our lighting His way and to show that we were prepared for His arrival. Frankly, all this symbolism bored me and I was usually daydreaming until she finally got around to talking about our new dresses. The five of us we who really couldn't care less about all that symbolic stuff would fake it through those meeting as if we were paying attention. It seemed to us like they were making a bigger deal about this than was necessary. After all, how hard could it be to light a lamp, hold it up, and be excited about watching Susan and Thad get married? Jael would get really mad at us when we didn't want to review that boring stuff with her and the other half of the Posse, but we didn't care. We figured it was no big deal. Nobody was going to be paying any real attention to us anyway. After the wedding, this little misunderstanding would all blow over.

Well, the big day finally came. We were at Jael's by 10 A.M. We got dressed and helped to get Susan ready. All of that was done by about 1 P.M. We were pretty nervous the whole time we were getting dressed, because we wanted to be ready when Thad got there to call for Susan. He had the option of showing up at any time. That was part of the excitement. I guess it was also symbolic of the fact that the Messiah could come at any time and we were supposed to be ready for Him. Jael and her side of the Posse were really antsy until everything was ready and she saw that we had made it before Thad showed up.

"Man, Jael is really trippin'," I commented to Simone.

"I know girl," Simone replied. "She's taking all the fun out of this."

"I know what you mean," Nila interjected. "She hassled me about everything from my shoes, to the bow in my hair, to the amount of oil I brought with me for my lamp."

"Yeah," Orpah joined in, "she harassed me about the oil too. What's the big deal? If she doesn't back off, she'll have this oil all over her head."

"You know how she is about this symbolism stuff." I replied.

"Really," Rachel said while smacking her gum, "as much as Thad loves Susan, he won't even wait until it gets dark to come and sweep her off of her feet. We'll probably be carrying these stupid lamps for nothing."

"They're not stupid lamps!" Oo-oh. Jael had overheard us. She came storming over to our little group enraged. Her eyes narrowed and her hands flew through the air as she accented every word. "You guys have not taken this whole thing seriously ever since you heard about the wedding. Now you're disrespecting my sister's most special day because you're ignorant to how important a role you hold. If you mess this up for Susan, I will never forgive you!"

"Cool out, Chick," I said, trying desperately to calm her down. I wanted to get her to lower her voice. She was making a scene. "Come over here and take a chill pill. Contrary to what you believe, we aren't trying to ruin Susan's day. That's just the point. It's Susan's day, not ours. This isn't about us and nobody is even paying us any attention. Relax. Everything will be fine."

"So you have your oil?" Jael questioned.

"Sure, sure. We're fine." I was doing my best to cover how annoyed I was by how ridiculous she was acting. "Now go on back over there with your mother and sister and do some wedding stuff. I tell you what, since you think we're not interested, we'll be responsible for watching out the window for Thad's arrival. Okay? We'll see him before you do. You'll see."

The rest of the afternoon went by smoothly. We had a light snack and began to settle down around 6 P.M. when Thad still hadn't shown up. Susan was waiting in another room, so we had no idea how she was handling the long wait. We were getting bored. By the time twilight came around, Nila had the bright idea of lighting our lamps and practicing carrying them up high enough to light the way for Thad. For once that day, all ten of us bridesmaids did something together. We paraded around in all sorts of different formations, deciding which would be the best to lead Thad to Susan and then to lead them to the wedding ceremony itself.

By 9:30 p.m., we were all getting sleepy because we had been up so long. Being excited uses up a lot of energy and we were fading fast. Pretty soon, we had all fallen asleep. All of a sudden, a shout was heard and someone yelled out, "The bridegroom is coming!" We woke up and ran to the sink to rinse our mouths and freshen our faces.

Then it happened! Amidst all the giggling, as the ten of us bridesmaids started to light our lamps, the five of us who had taken the whole thing lightly realized we were out of oil. We had used it all up during our practice. Leave it to Jael and her crew to have thought about buying extra oil for their lamps. They each had a whole new cruse.

"Jael, you've got to help us," we begged. "We used up all our oil during our practice time earlier this evening. Let us use a little of yours."

"I told you so, I told you so," accused Jael through narrowed eyes. "Too bad. If we give you ours, we won't have enough for ourselves to last for the whole ceremony. You'd better try to wake up old Mr. Joseph and see if he will get up and sell you some more. We don't have time to fool around with you. Our five lamps will just have to be enough. We figured something like this might happen, so the five of us prepared to light the way for Thad without you. Good luck with Mr. Joseph. He's mean during the day; I wouldn't want to tangle with him in the middle of the night."

And with that, she, Carmen, Deborah, Liz, and Rita took off. We could hear all the glad voices and see the glimmer of their lamps as they descended the steps to the street out front. We hurried out the back door, tripping over and dirtying the hems of our beautiful dresses, and down the walk in the dark to Mr. Joseph's shop to see what we could do at this hour about our need for oil. Although we rushed, we all knew we had really messed up and would never make it back in time. We should have listened. We should have prepared, but we didn't. We would never have that same opportunity again.

It's easy to get carried away with daydreams. Movies, stage plays, and classic literature are full of tales of fortunes gained and lost and beautiful love stories. Many times, it's only in biographies (which aren't that popular) that we find out about the background of hard work it took for that fortune to be accumulated or that love to be sustained.

You are probably at a place in your life right now where you are thinking about your future. If you haven't given your future that much thought, you probably have parents and teachers who are trying their best to impress upon you the importance of settling down and getting serious. High school graduation looms in front of you as do college applications and SAT's or ACT's. You could be thinking about the possibilities of moving away from home and living on your own. Maybe you're looking forward to getting a job and making your own money. All of this may be exciting to you or it may be a little scary.

An old saying states, "If you fail to plan, you plan to fail." What are you going to do with your future? How can you plan? How can you be sure that the things you don't want to happen, won't happen?

DO THIS: Use the following activity to help you dodge the possibility of being like one of the five foolish girls. After you have thought through these issues, have a Christian friend or mentor to read and initial your plan. Give this person permission to ask you how you are doing in each area. (In other words, allow this person to hold you accountable for your actions that may affect your plan.)

THINGS I *DON'T* WANT TO HAPPEN TO ME	HOW I PLAN TO KEEP AWAY FROM THIS	INITIALS
Example: I don't want to become a teen parent.	I will practice celibacy until I get married. I will participate in group dating. I will let my dates know about my commitment to celibacy. I will hold my virginity in high esteem.	
1.		
2.		
3.		

THINGS I HOPE FOR MY FUTURE.	HOW I PLAN TO MAKE THIS HAPPEN.	INITIALS
1. My 6-month plan		
2. My 1-year plan		
3. My 3-year plan		
4. My 5-year plan		
5. My 10-year plan		

MEMORY VERSE FOR THE "UNDISCIPLINED FOOLISH GIRLS"

Ps. 37:37–38 Consider the blameless, observe the upright; there is a future for the man of peace. But all sinners will be destroyed; the future of the wicked will be cut off. (NIV)

Not Taken Seriously

JOASH/JEHOASH

2 Kings 11–12:1–6 and 2 Chr. 22:10–24:14
I will honor God, even if my family, friends, and others do not.

You think your family has problems? Ha! Please. If there were a prize being given out for the most dysfunctional family on the planet, mine would win hands down. A lot of people I know who have families half as messed up as mine have gone crazy. Some of those people are tripping out on drugs, running with the wrong people, or just wasting their lives away feeling sorry for themselves. I decided I wasn't going to let any of these things happen to me, regardless of the crazy folks that surrounded me. The comment was probably made that nothing good could ever come from my family. My name is Joash. Let me tell you my story.

My dad was a king. His name was Ahaziah. Our family came from a long line of kings and I understand that it was always a big deal to know who the next king would be after the present one died. So you can imagine, there was always a lot of kissing-up and behind-the-back stuff going on. Normally, the king's oldest son would be the obvious choice for who would take the king's place, but with kings marrying more than one woman, and having kids by them, those kids were usually being played against each other. The mothers, brothers, aunts, and uncles would get involved too.

I lived during the time when God's people were divided into two kingdoms, Israel and Judah. My family was the royal family of Judah. My great-grandfather, Jehoshaphat, was a righteous king who tried to make friends with Ahab who was the king of Israel at the time. They did some stuff together, but things didn't work out well enough to reunite the kingdom or anything. King Ahab was a real bad actor and basically kicked God to the curb in favor of the false God, Baal. Great-granddaddy Jehoshaphat wasn't hearing that, so he tried to keep Judah separated from the sins that had gotten out of control in Israel.

Still, I think it may have been because of Great-granddaddy's friendship with Ahab, that my grandfather, Jehoram, ended up marrying one of Ahab's daughters, Athaliah. You know how a guy can get when he is trying to please a woman. Well, Granddaddy Jehoram chucked God trying to stay cool with his wife and his in-laws rather than with his own God. Stupid.

Anyway, Grandma Athaliah was trying to run everybody's lives while both Judah (the kingdom my family ruled) and Israel were going to the dogs. Granddaddy Jehoram ruled Judah for only eight years, but Grandma Athaliah wasn't about to give up her power in the royal scheme of things. Her son, Ahaziah, my dad, became king and his mom was never too far from the throne room.

In the meantime, the junk happening over in Israel continued. King Ahab had stolen this guy's field and murdered him behind it and the Queen, Jezebel, was keeping up her own confusion ordering the prophets of Baal around and giving the God's prophet Elijah a hard time. All their sin was getting them in deeper and deeper trouble with God.

My dad was considered to have been an evil king like his daddy, and with the two royal families connected by marriage, he started hanging around with Joram, the new king over in Israel. They must have thought they were bad because my dad and Joram decided to attack the enemy, Hazael king of Aram, together. The enemy ended up wounding King Joram, so he got out of the fight. My dad, King Ahaziah, went to visit his friend while he was sick and that's when stuff really hit the fan.

God had basically had enough of the sins of both kingdoms. It was time for Him to punish Ahab, Jezebel, Athaliah, and all the rest who had encouraged the worship of Baal over Him. He told the prophet Elisha to anoint a new king over Israel. Jehu, one of my great-uncles, was chosen. Well, of course, the royal family of Israel wasn't at all excited about having a descendent of the royal family of Judah over them, so this whole thing had to be done on the Q. T. Not only that, but once Jehu was anointed king, God told him to kill everybody who was a member of the Ahab's family.

Great-uncle Jehu had no problem with that order from the Lord. He and his men went after King Joram first. Jehu boldly drove his chariot straight into the city where Joram was recuperating. (As they looked out of their window, Joram and Ahaziah saw him coming because they recognized his crazy driving.) They tried to get away, but Jehu personally speared Joram, killing him in his chariot as he tried to make a run for it. (Joram was buried in the very field that his dad had stolen from Naboth years before.) My dad was shot too. He died in the city of Megiddo and was buried in the family plot.

Of course, you know what that meant. There needed to be a new king in Judah. When Grandma Athaliah found out that her baby, my dad Ahaziah, had been killed, she decided that none of his other relatives should be rule Judah. I guess she figured she could run it herself if all the male descendants of the royal line were gone. So while Jehu was still killing the descendants of Ahab over in Israel (he killed Jezebel, Ahab's 70 sons, and all the worshippers of Baal), Athaliah began her own search and destroy mission to kill all the royals of Judah. (See, I told you I came from a dysfunctional family.)

I was only a few months old when the stuff got to this point. Thankfully, my aunt Jehosheba was married to the priest Jehoiada and she was a God-fearing woman. This aunt grabbed me and hid me in the temple of God. She hid me for six years! Finally, Priest Jehoiada got up his courage, gathered the agreement of the commanders of Judah, brought me out, and anointed me as king of Judah. I was only seven years old.

When Grandma Athaliah heard the noise of the people cheering because I was king, she was so mad she started to scream and tear her clothes up. Besides me, she was the last one of the family still alive. Jehoiada had her killed and there was a big celebration.

Now, of course, for quite a few years, Jehoiada ran the government along with the commanders and other priests, because I was so young. However, he was training me to take over and to take my place as king. Once I reached my teens and under the guidance of God's priest, I felt I knew what I wanted to do. I wanted to be sure to keep Judah focused on the true God because I had seen what could happen when God got angry about His people worshipping other gods.

With that in mind, my first order was to restore the temple of God. Do you know all those priests (except Jehoiada) simply ignored me. All the way through my teens, they just refused to do what I asked them to do. How could priests refuse to repair the temple? That didn't make any sense to me. I finally figured that it was because of my age that they didn't honor me. "Ain't that a blip," I thought. But since I knew I was right, I just kept on bugging them. I was determined to get things done for God, even if the adults refused to help me.

It wasn't until Joash had reigned for 23 years before the priests began to take up the collection to finance the repair of the temple. And that still didn't happen until Joash begged Jehoiada to speak to the priests for him.

Many times, teens who are trying to do the right thing are not taken seriously. You may be the only one in your family who is a Christian. You may be dealing with adults in your family who are involved with drugs and/or alcohol. Maybe you are protecting yourself and perhaps younger brothers and sisters from physical abuse. It could be that an adult is trying to encourage or even force you into involvement with sex.

If that's you, don't be discouraged. Look at how Joash was able to be different from his ungodly family. In the same way that Joash had Jehoiada to help him, you need to seek help from a Christian adult. A loving pastor, teacher, professional counselor, or other family member would be happy to assist you. God is able to give you the strength to stand up for what's right, no matter who is ignoring you or saying you're wrong.

DO THIS: Some things you are facing may be very difficult issues that you wish you didn't have to face. You may even feel you are being forced to grow up too fast. Following the examples given, use the chart below to think and pray through some of your or your friends' problems.

Issue	Bible Encouragement	Prayer	My Standing Statement	My Plan t Get Help
Ex. 1 - My mom is using cocaine	1 Cor 6:19-20 Do you not know that your body is a temple of the Holy Spirit... Therefore honor God with your body. NIV	Lord, help my mom to realize her body is your temple so she will put the right things in it.	I will stay away from drugs.	Ask the pasto to speak wit her.
Ex. 2 - My uncle has forced me to do sexual things with him.	Matt 5:28 But I tell you that anyone who looks at a woman lustfully has already committed adultery with her in his heart. NIV	Lord, please protect me from my uncle until someone helps me escape his advances.	I will not blame myself for the abuses forced upon me. I will not consent to impurity.	Report th sexual abus to authorities

MEMORY VERSE FOR "NOT TAKEN SERIOUSLY JOASH"

Gal. 2:20 I have been crucified with Christ and I no longer live, but Christ lives in me. The life I live in the body, I live by faith in the Son of God, who loved me and gave himself for me. (NIV)

Chapter 14

Impatient

Lot's Daughters

Gen. 19:30–38

We will not wait for God to provide for us.

My sister and I grew up in what you would probably call a stable home. We had both our father and mother with us and we were pretty well off. As a matter of fact, our great-uncle Abraham had been especially chosen and blessed by God. From the very beginning of Uncle Abe's special relationship with God, our father Lot had been right by his side.

You can probably imagine what it's like to be the relatives of an important person or a celebrity. Sometimes, people are just as interested in you as they are in the real star. It was sort of like that for my younger sister and me. Dad was always telling us we had to watch how we acted because people were looking at us. Mom didn't put quite as much pressure on us about this. I guess it was because she hadn't been with Uncle Abraham as long as our dad had and she didn't really think Uncle Abe was all that big of a deal. Actually, she thought he got way too much credit for stuff and she wanted Dad to just get his own recognition.

That recognition started to come our dad's way when we were living in Sodom. Dad had an important job with the leaders of the city and mom was really pleased. She was one of those society ladies who liked the attention she received because of dad's position. She was proud of her house and she liked the excitement of the city. She treated us like little dolls, dressing us up and showing us off so all the other society ladies could ooh and aah over us. We grew up living pretty charmed and privileged lives.

When we finally reached our teens, like all the other girls our age, we were interested in guys. As the oldest, I was expected to find a boyfriend first. It seemed to take an unusually long time to find someone interesting and who was interested in me, but I finally got together with a guy and he became my boyfriend. Strangely, my sister had the same problem I had, but finally she started going steady with a guy too.

We were happy about our boyfriends, but most of the guys we knew didn't really hang out with girls much. We thought they were just being normal, stupid guys, wanting to hang around each other, play basketball, talk about sports, and scratch themselves. But pretty soon we began to realize that there was something stranger about most of the guys and men in Sodom.

Everything became clear the day the strangers arrived. That particular afternoon, Dad brought these two strangers home with him from work. I remember they were really tall and muscular. I mean these guys were built. Anyway, Dad invited them in and while Mom was rushing around trying to be hospitable, a crowd gathered right outside our house. They began to bang on the door and ask our father to send the strangers out to them. Dad then did a very strange thing. He offered *us* to the men. Us, my sister and me. It finally dawned on us why the guys in the city were never really interested in girls. Turns out, Sodom was well-known as the homosexual capital of the whole region. That crowd had wanted to get with those strangers and they weren't even interested in our dad's offer of two virgins to dissuade them.

We sure didn't want to go out into that crowd, but before we even had a chance to get scared or protest, the strangers had pulled Dad back into the house, locked the door, and did something to that crowd to make them go away. As we peaked out of the window, we could see the men leaving our house, feeling their way through the streets as if they were suddenly blind! It was weird. The strangers told my dad we had to move out tomorrow because God was going to do something really bad to the whole city.

Well, Mom wasn't even hearing that. Leave her house and her society thing? No way. But the men were so adamant, that they convinced our dad.

"Girls, you have to spend the evening packing. We are leaving tomorrow for a little while. Don't ask any questions, just pack one bag and be ready to leave in the morning."

Don't ask any questions? How were we supposed to know what to pack? And just one bag? He was crazy. Mom was full of questions but he just kept telling her not to ask, just trust him on this one.

Well, the morning came and the men returned first thing. We had no idea how long we were going to be gone or where we were going for that matter, so we all kept changing our minds about what to take and what to leave. I guess we were taking too long because finally, the strangers grabbed our hands and hustled us out the door, down the main street, and through the front gate of the city. People were looking at us really strangely but no one else seemed to be alarmed. We were the only ones running as if there was a fire. Frankly, we felt pretty stupid and I wondered what we would say to everybody when we came back. Even in the rush, I especially thought about my boyfriend and all the plans we had made. Would he want me after this embarrassing episode?

I tuned back in while we were still rushing along just in time to hear the strangers warn us saying, "Run for your lives! Don't stop until you are safely in the mountains, and whatever you do, don't look back!"

We were scared now. It was just the way they said it, you knew they meant something terrible would happen if we did. Still, even in the middle of our rush and our fear, we were extremely curious about what was going to happen in the city.

Dad pleaded with the men. "Please," Dad said, "don't make us run to the mountains. I'm afraid the disaster will reach me there. Listen, there's a little town not far from here. Zoar. Let me go there and then I can be assured that I won't die."

What did Dad mean by saying that the disaster wouldn't reach *him* and let *him* run to the little city? It sounded to us like he was leaving us completely out of his escape plan. *Ain't that nothin'*, I thought.

The men answered, "All right, all right. You can go to Zoar, but get there in a hurry. Nothing can happen until you are safe, but if you wait too long, you won't be. Now go!"

The men stayed behind and we all kept running. Dad was in front with our mom close behind him; my sister and I were a little behind her. Then we heard the first explosion. It was like nothing we had ever heard before. It seemed like the explosion blew Dad further ahead because he really took off then. My sister and I were just kicking it into second gear when we saw our mom suddenly turn and look back. It only took a quick, split second. There was a weird expression on her face like she really missed everything she had left behind, and then she wasn't a real person anymore. By the time we reached the spot where she was, all we could do was stare and scream. She was a statue. My sister reached out to touch her hand and granules flaked off. She was salt.

We heard two or three more explosions. There was nothing we could do but keep running and trying to catch up with our father. Once we did, we didn't talk. We just kept on running until we got to Zoar.

The next 24 hours was a blur. We were a mess of emotions—confused and grief—stricken about what had happened to our mother, lonely for and worrying about our boyfriends, and mad at yet still dependent upon our dad. Once we figured out that God had destroyed Sodom because of its sin, we only stayed in Zoar that day and left the next, because we saw some of the men there who had the same problem as Sodom's men had had. So Dad moved us to the mountains after all, saying that he knew he had to obey what God had originally intended for him to do.

As we huddled together at night, trying to keep warm in our tent, my sister and I had some long whispered talks.

"I'm cold, I'm lonely, I'm sad, and I'm scared," my little sister complained one night.

"I know, Sis," I answered. "We've got to make the best of this because we are all we have."

"That scares me even more. What's going to happen to us? We have no future with old scared-y-cat over there. He wouldn't help mom, now he doesn't even want to live in a city."

"Yeah, I think he's way over the top, but there is something we can do."

"What? I'll do anything to get out of this stupid tent."

"We can start families. Then Dad will have to let us move back to a city. He wouldn't want us to raise kids out here in the wilderness."

"Wake up, Big Sister. There are no men out here. I may not know much, but I know it takes two to have a baby."

"Open your eyes, Lil Sis. There is one man out here."

"Dad? Big S., you've lost it now."

"No, listen. Dad didn't have any boys, right?"

"Right."

"His heritage will die if he doesn't have any sons and Mom's gone so he won't have any now, right?"

"Right."

"He's not moving back to a city, so the only way he has a possibility of having sons is if we give him some."

"Wake up. We still don't have husbands."

"The law says that if a man dies and his wife didn't give him any heirs, the dead husband's brother can get with the widow and give her a baby that she will raise as her husband's heir. What's the difference here? We'll just be doing what mom would do if she was here. We'll get busy with Dad and raise heirs for him."

"Believe it or not, even though I've never heard of it working this way, I can see your point. Besides, we will probably get old and crusty waiting to see if Dad ever changes his mind about living in a city again. We will probably never have husbands. I'm in. But how are we going to convince Dad to go along with this?

"We won't convince him. We'll sneak back into town, buy booze, get him drunk, and do our thing while he's out of it."

"Sounds like a plan. Let's do it."

The impatience of Lot's daughters led to both girls being pregnant by their father. Like any other time when impatience is allowed to rule your actions, something very negative takes place. The two babies that were born, Moab and Benammi, became fathers of nations that caused God's people much heartache and trouble. Lot's daughters had no idea what would happen in the days to come. Trusting God, regardless of what is going on at the present time, always leaves room for faith in a better future.

Why does it seem so hard to wait for anything? Two of the biggest problems that teenagers have when it comes to patience are in the areas of sex and money. You want to have sex right now and you want lots of money right now. Young people of every race and class are engaging in premarital sex. The negative consequences are evident in the continued levels of young pregnancies and numbers of youth who have contracted sexually transmitted diseases. The gang problem mainly exists because of the lucrative nature of drug trafficking. And more and more young men are neglecting or postponing college in favor of accepting basketball careers which may or may not last.

Think about a time when you were impatient and you rushed into something. Usually when you rush in, you end up in trouble. You probably didn't even consider all the negative things that could happen if you carried out your impatient plan. All you knew was that it was hard to wait for what you really, really wanted.

DO THIS: Evaluate some of the things you really want on the following chart.

List what you really want.	Why do you want this?	List negatives that could happen if you receive this.	List positive things you can do while you wait.

Name one or two positive things about patience.

_____

_____

MEMORY VERSE FOR "IMPATIENT LOT'S DAUGHTERS"

Eccl. 7:8 The end of a matter is better than its beginning, and patience is better than pride. (NIV)

Headstrong

JESUS

Luke 2: 40–52
I will not neglect God's business.

My name is Jesus. I am from a little unimportant town called Nazareth. My dad, Joseph, is a carpenter and my mom, Mary, is a homemaker. I have two younger brothers, James and Jude and Mom hopes to have a couple of girls someday too. Dad is teaching us boys his carpentry trade, but I have a feeling I won't be going into the family business. That feeling has come about because of what my parents have told me about the circumstances that surrounded my birth, and something that happened just as I was entering my teen years. If I don't tell you about the first thing, you won't understand the second.

Have you ever heard your mom or dad or grandmother or someone tell you about the circumstances surrounding your birth? Most guys our age probably wouldn't admit this, but I like to hear my story. Hearing it gives me a good feeling—like I was really wanted. I've had friends who didn't know their story and there always seemed to be something missing for them. Anyway, all of that is beside the point. Let me get back on track.

Like I said, I like to tell the story about how I was born. This story is very much like my personality—very unbelievable, surprising, and headstrong. I think a story can be headstrong if lots of people don't believe it but those who are part of the story refuse to change it. I actually can't tell it too much, because I want to keep Mom and Dad from being laughed at. They don't deserve for their integrity to always be questioned.

You see, my mom became pregnant with me while she was engaged to my dad. I know, you may be thinking, "Big deal. That happens to people all the time." Well, back in the day when I was born, if a young Jewish girl got pregnant before she was married, she could possibly have received the death penalty. Everyone took it that seriously. The thing was, she insisted that she was still a virgin. She said an angel had brought her the message from God that she would be the mother of the promised Messiah. In order for that to happen, she had to have been a virgin so that the baby would be God's son, not some human man's son.

You can probably imagine the conversation between my mom and dad when she told him that she was pregnant. At first, he didn't believe her. He loved her and was pretty upset and extremely disappointed because he thought she had been getting busy with some other guy. He knew what it took to get pregnant and he knew he hadn't touched my mom like that. It took another angelic message, to him this time, to convince him that my mom was telling the truth. After that, because God had given them direct messages, it didn't matter who didn't believe them. They stuck to that story. It was pretty headstrong of them to insist that the birth of their first son was due to a miracle that came directly from God, so I don't feel so bad about my own headstrong tendencies. I get it from my parents. All three of them—Mom, Dad, and God—are pretty determined in how they think and operate.

Okay, so now that you know my birth story, you know that I am the Messiah. Pretty cool, huh? Don't get excited though. I won't be taking my place as the Messiah until I'm grown. It's kind of like if your parents have an inheritance waiting for you and they own a business. When you get to be 18 or 21, or when they die, you will receive the money and begin to run the business. When you're twelve or thirteen, although you know who you are and you know what's coming, you can't cash in on anything yet. That's one way I can describe this Messiah thing to you. I am He, but I won't be operating as Him until I get older.

Knowing who you are and where you're headed should make a difference in some of the things you get into though. For example, if you're going to be a doctor, you're probably really interested in science. You would probably love to go to nerdy science camps and you try to keep your grades up so you can get into med school. If you expect to be a pro basketball player, you will protect your knees and sign up every summer to play in the YMCA league. Well, although my life was pretty much like most other kids' lives my age, I was already doing some things that indicated who I would become. One of those incidents happened when I was twelve-years-old, right around the time I would have my Bar Mitzvah, the ceremony that labeled me "a man".

Our family would go up to Jerusalem every year for the Feast of the Passover. This year was special, because I was twelve and wouldn't be considered a little kid anymore. The vacation went pretty much as usual. We celebrated the Feast and visited all the usual places while we were in town. This time though, I was drawn to the temple. Every day I walked around it and through it. I watched the people bring in their animals, grain, and wine. I watched the priests do the sacrifices in the outer court. I also watched as the priests went in and out, to and from whatever meetings they were having. I just had to know what was going on with them.

I finally got up the courage to speak to one of the priests. The guy had a real serious face but it looked kinda friendly, what I could see of it behind his beard. My questions must have really surprised him because he invited me to their next meeting. I was so excited that I didn't even go tell my parents where I would be. I just had enough time to eat a little lunch before the meeting began.

Inside their meeting chamber, I listened as they had prayers and then began to discuss the Scriptures. I had been in Hebrew school like every other good Jewish boy, so I was familiar with the passages they were discussing. I started asking them some of the questions my Hebrew school teachers had been unable to answer for me. The conversation was so exciting that we didn't even notice how late it had gotten. I ended up staying there for several days. The other thing I didn't notice was that it was the day my family would begin to travel back to Nazareth. I just kept on listening, asking questions, and discussing my opinion with the priests. They all seemed amazed by my questions and answers and they kept on asking new people into the meetings to join our discussions.

I didn't know how long I had been there when all of a sudden I looked up and there were my mom and dad. They had that stressed look on their faces that parents get when you know you're about to get into trouble. Mom rushed over to me and grabbed me in a huge hug. I was totally confused because she was crying.

"Son, why have you done this to us?" she asked. "Don't you realize that we've been searching for you for three days? You had us worried sick."

My dad chimed in, "Boy, we had already started on the trip home. We thought you were in the caravan along with some of your cousins or something. We had gotten a day's journey out of town before we noticed that you were not with anybody. We came back immediately and have been going crazy trying to find you."

It seemed so obvious to me that the temple should have been the first place they looked that I couldn't understand where else they may have gone. "Why were you looking in a bunch of different places? Didn't it occur to you that if you couldn't find me, I would be in my Father's house?"

I could tell by their faces that they didn't understand what I meant, but that was beside the point. I knew what I had to do. I had to go home with them and keep on being their kid until it was time for me to take my place in God's plan. So that's what I did. I went home.

Headstrong

Even Jesus had to obey His parents. Yes, he was headstrong. He knew who He was and what He had to do, and nothing was going to stop Him. He also knew when it was the right time to do what He had to do. As a Christian, you too must be headstrong about your faith. You're young and you have plenty of energy to be able to work enthusiastically for the Lord. You are also bold and this boldness gives you the courage to proclaim your faith and act on what God wants you to do.

DO THIS: Witnessing, sharing your faith with your friends, is one of the most important things you can do. Think of three to five friends who are not Christians. List their names below. In the box next to each name, plan an opening line you will use to start talking to him or her about the Lord. In the last box, write a date on which you will talk to each friend. Be sure to end each conversation by asking if that friend would like to know more about God and possibly become more involved with the church. When you get a yes answer, follow through by inviting that friend to church.

Friend's Name	Opening Line	Contact Date

MEMORY VERSE FOR "HEADSTRONG JESUS"

1 Cor. 15:58 Therefore, my dear brothers, stand firm. Let nothing move you. Always give yourselves fully to the work of the Lord, because you know that your labor in the Lord is not in vain. (NIV)

Contact Information

REDEMPTION
PRESS

To order additional copies of this book, please visit
www.redemption-press.com.
Also available on Amazon.com and BarnesandNoble.com
Or by calling toll free 1-844-2REDEEM

CPSIA information can be obtained at www.ICGtesting.com
Printed in the USA
LVOW04s1556060515

437463LV00018B/810/P